GOD-
BIRTHING

GOD-
BIRTHING

TOWARD
SACREDNESS,
PERSONAL MEANING,
AND SPIRITUAL
NOURISHMENT

Michael Dwinell

Triumph™ Books
Liguori, Missouri

Published by Triumph™ Books
Liguori, Missouri 63057-9999
An Imprint of Liguori Publications

Library of Congress Cataloging-in-Publication Data

Dwinell, Michael.
    God-birthing: a guide to sacredness, personal
meaning, and spiritual nourishment / Michael Dwinell.
            p.   cm.
    Includes bibliographical references.
    ISBN 0-89243-640-9
    1. Spiritual life—Christianity. 2. Dwinell, Michael.
I. Title. BV4501.2.D88   1994
248.4—dc20
                                        94-5178
                                        CIP

Copyright © 1994 by Michael Dwinell
Printed in the United States of America
First Edition

Dedication

○○○○○○○○○○○○○○

To all those known and unknown,
    named and unnamed,
    dear to me and stranger,
who have trusted their instincts,
    their bodies, their dreams
to be bearers of the Word—
who have dared to know that the Word
    in Scripture
    is but the first word
    spoken continually by the breath
of the Son unto this very moment and beyond
    through each of us—
    God's Becoming.

February 20, 1994

Contents

ooooooooooooooo

With special thanks to
Viki and Carol, Kathleen,
Emily, Joan, and John.

Introduction

ⲟⲟⲟⲟⲟⲟⲟⲟⲟⲟⲟⲟⲟⲟⲟⲟ

IN AS MUCH as this book attempts to set forth a knowing of God as the Holy One whose on-going birthing takes place in and through the individual and collective lives of human beings, it seems fitting to begin by reflecting upon the birthing process within me that produced this book. There has been in me a lifelong process of gestation, and now, finally, a birthing that culminates in the knowing that the most important and accurate way to describe and understand human life is to name it "God-birthing": "Theogenesis."

From what birth comes this book? What are some of the moments of conception that give birth to a book *God-Birthing?*

Ogunquit, Maine, was so named by the Indians—a name meaning "a place beautiful by the sea." It still is, and its white sandy beach is even more so. It is a place to which I had come every summer for the first twenty-five years, a place that had always been for me full with God.

On that day, forty-five years ago, the ocean was triumphantly and magnificently violent; it was the day after a hurricane. I ventured as close to the water as possible, watching, entranced by the waves, the wind, the sounds, the wetness in the air, the smell of ocean everywhere. Behind me stood my mother and her mother, my grandmother. My grandmother was a woman of genuine charity and the passion of unconditional love; she meant a great deal to me. She whispered to my mother, thinking that I could not hear—but because she was deaf, her voice carried over the waves: "When he grows up, he is going to be a priest."

I was too young to know what the word *priest* meant, but somehow I did know that my grandmother was right, absolutely right. She had seen me through and through. She saw me seeing something in that ocean. She saw me struck with reverence and awe. She knew that I knew that we were in the presence of the Holy. I had been seen through and through, and her words went through me, through and through.

And thus it has always been for me. I cannot remember a time when I have not known experience as the becoming of the Holy. My grandmother saw true, spoke true, both then and now.

From what birth comes this book? Not long after I graduated from seminary and was settled in my first job as an assistant in a well-to-do suburban, white, southern parish, I encountered a powerful ethical dilemma.

Martin Luther King had been shot, and the evening of his death, the vestry (the lay leadership of the church) met. Among that group, there was talk of passing a resolution thanking God for this man's death. While the talk never reached the stage of a formal motion, it was taken seriously and nobody made significant objection. I felt a desperate need to speak, to speak out, to shout my disbelief that this conversation could go on in a church that professed Jesus the Christ as Lord. I even thought that perhaps I should resign. But I was young, fresh out of seminary, married, with one small child. Mostly I was just plain scared! I didn't say a word. But I was haunted, and I did wonder. I wondered if the time would ever come when I would dare to speak, to proclaim the truth as it had been given to me with no holds barred, with no punches pulled.

From what birth comes this book? June 1993 marked the twenty-fifth anniversary of my ordination to priesthood, and although I have struggled with the institutional Church and traditional religion, I have been immersed in and saturated by Scripture and liturgy. Scripture and liturgy have been, indeed, formative, formidable, and incredibly demanding—demanding more than curiosity and intriguedness. Scripture and liturgy have been, for me, compelling, not because they are "religious." I don't think they are particularly "religious" anyway. Rather, they raise up the most significant questions about the meaning and nature of the mystery of our existence.

For instance, when we celebrate Eucharist and hear the words, "Do this in remembrance of me," the question always comes to my mind, *Do what?* Is Jesus asking us simply to remember to invoke his name when we break bread? Is that all? Or is there something else? *Do what?* To what exactly are we commanded, or perhaps, invited?

I also question: In the Garden of Gethsemane where Jesus wrestles in anguish with what is to come, making it clear that he is not the victim of Roman authorities or Jewish religious hierarchy, but rather that he is making a conscious, intentional, voluntary, and willing act of surrender to God's will, to God's need—what, then, is the necessary urgency within the Godhead itself that requires Jesus' crucifixion?

The questions are intriguing and compelling. This book comes out of years of saturation in the compellingness of Scripture and liturgy.

From what birth comes this book? "Thou shalt love the Lord, thy God, with all thy heart, with all thy soul, and with all thy mind. This is the first and great commandment. And the second is like unto it: thou shalt love thy neighbor as thyself." These are magnificent words—and only recently have I heard them as I have never heard them before. For years, I have heard them as an order, a command, an obligation, a requirement, a duty, a guilt-fermenting expectation of perfection that was obviously never achievable.

Then quite suddenly, I began to hear these words differently. Instead of being a command, they became an invitation and a prophecy. If you know God—not know about God—you will come to love God with everything that you are. If you know God, you will not be able to help but love God. If you know God, you will discover yourself loving yourself and your neighbor. If you know God, you will come to love God with everything you are even to the point, perhaps, of saying "Yes" in the Garden of Gethsemane.

What is this knowing and loving of God? What is there about the experience of God that moves us to love so profoundly that we are willing to be used by God as God's own birthing point—perhaps to the point of surrendering our very lives?

From what birth comes this book? In the words of Meister Echkart:

> From all eternity
> God lies on a maternity bed
>   giving birth.
> The essence of God is birthing.
>
> We are all meant
>   to be mothers of God.
>> *Meditations With Meister Eckhart*

ooooooooooooooo

In the words of Teilhard de Chardin:

> So, it is no longer simply a matter of seeing God
> and allowing one's self to be enveloped
> and penetrated by God—
> we have to do more:
> we have to disclose God

(for even in one sense of the word
   "complete" God)
   ever more fully....
God is in the process of "changing"
As a result of the coincidence
   of God's magnetic power
and our own thought.

Meditations With Teilhard de Chardin

○○○○○○○○○○○○○○○

And, finally, in the words of a five-year old:

Please help God.
He is getting born
and everything in the world
you have God.

Poem of a five-year-old

○○○○○○○○○○○○○○○

Whether it be the words of the thirteenth-century male adult mystic or of a five-year-old child living in New Hampshire in 1993, the truth of this book is not new. It is imbedded in history. It is imbedded in Scripture. It is imbedded in the presence of the human heart. Having life is God-birthing.

From what birth comes this book? Finally, this book comes out of listening to hundreds of people talk about their lives; listening to what they have said, what they haven't said; what they've said with their eyes, their bodies, in their creative work; listening to their hearts, listening to the confusion and the anguish. You tell me about the dilemmas and crises in your lives. You tell me about your history and your families. You tell me things you have never told anyone else. You experience relief and insight. You make wonderful and creative changes in your lives. You find things to do with your lives that are fulfilling and satisfying. Yet, after all that, you still find yourselves plagued with one question, and you have the generosity and courage of spirit to ask that question not just for yourself but for all humanity. How often have I heard one of you say, "After all this, I still don't know what the point is. What is the point? Even if we feed the people in Somalia and stop the war in Bosnia, what is the point? What is the point of the human condition, the human experience, the human mystery? How do you, how do I, how do we find value? How do we find value in it all? No matter how well my life goes," you say, "I remain in anguish until I have some sense of the value of it all."

You are asking the right question—ultimately, the only question—and this book is about that question.

How can we look the reality of human existence and human experience right in the eye, and unflinchingly comprehend its agony and terror and brutality, while at the same time give wholehearted and unreserved affirmation of life's value.

The answer: Understanding human living is, in fact, nothing less than the labor pains of God's becoming.

This book is an attempt to proclaim, to paint, to evoke that vision and that hope.

I

ooooooooooooooo

THE
EXPERIENCE
OF REALITY

ooooooooooooooo

Dear Daughter Elise,

I BEGIN BY WRITING YOU a letter. I write this letter because I both need to and want to. I have known God, experienced God, for a long time. In fact, I cannot remember a time when I have not experienced God. The struggle in me to become clear about, and more importantly, to be able to articulate my understanding and knowing of God has been long. It has been longer than you have been alive. This book is an attempt to put into words some of the fruits of that inner wrestling toward clarity—a wrestling that is not yet finished. I hope it never is.

In the adventure of writing about this wonderful struggle, I need to speak in a vulnerable and quiet voice. I need to speak to someone I love, to someone I know loves me and is already thinking about some of the ideas I write about. Thus, Elise, I write to you, my eldest child.

My perceptions of God are not particularly academic. They are much more perceived through the imagination of the heart. Intellect, of course, has been helpful to me in clarifying what I know not to be true, but heart-knowing has revealed the way to what demands to be affirmed. So, I need to speak personally and gently from my heart. And since we, in the past, have already begun to speak that way, why not continue.

> *You have placed me before Your ultimate mystery, oh God. I am grateful to You for that. I even have the strength to accept it and to know that there is no answer. That we must be able to bear your mysteries.*
>
> *An Interrupted Life: The Diaries of Etty Hillesum, 1941–1943*

Dear Elise,

I N HIS MOST POPULAR BOOK, *The Road Less Traveled*, M. Scott Peck begins by saying, "Life is difficult." Actually, Elise, it's much worse than that! Buddah's words upon his enlightenment are more accurate: "Behold, the world is monstrous suffering!"

You and I were lucky enough to be born at a particular time into a particular family, which means we were protected from many of life's horrors. But even so, you and I both know of the pain and sorrow and suffering and struggle that goes with being a human being.

Throughout the history of the human race, including now, the experience of living has been extremely difficult. A huge variety of external conditions have always ravaged us—not the least of which is the extraordinary depraved aggressiveness of this world's most cunning predator, our fellow human being. We not only savage one another, however. Because we must contend with a whole myriad of internal psychological difficulties, we savage ourselves as well. As the Psalmist alluded, "We have been made less than the angel and more than the animal." In fact, we have a good dose of both animal and angel in us, and they don't live very well with each other! Our inner life is one of conflict, tension, and insolvable paradoxes that take us from the heights to the depths and produce the most exhilarating and miserable and oppressive mood swings.

I could go on, Elise, but Buddah is right: To be a human being is to suffer, and nobody escapes. Furthermore, we endure all this with a sure and certain knowledge that we will die; perhaps later than sooner, but we will surely die. There are those writers who say that the terror of our certain mortality is the worst condition of our existence, and in fact, it is this very tenor which drives all human culture and civilization.

Yet and still, in the face of all that, we human beings survive; we love and make love, and bear and raise children, and hope. Sometimes we even act with inspirational courage and bless the world with incredible beauty.

But most of all, we are consumed with both the need and the desire to "make sense" of our condition, to understand it, and perhaps by understanding it, to escape it—and if not to escape it, at least to alleviate it.

We human beings are drawn to and fascinated by—out of necessity and perhaps in response to a sense of adventure—seeking to penetrate the mystery of our existence in the hope of gaining some understanding that will make our lives less painful and threatening, less difficult and demoralizing. Perhaps human life has some meaning in the ultimate sense. It might be connected to something important in the universe.

> *I now realize, God, how much You have given me. So much that was beautiful and so much that was hard to bear. Yet, whenever I showed myself ready to bear it, the hard was directly transformed into the beautiful.*
>
> *And the beautiful was sometimes much harder to bear, so overpowering did it seem. To think that one small human heart can experience so much, oh God, so much suffering and so much love, I am grateful to You, God, for having chosen my heart, in these times, to experience all the things it has experienced.*
>
> An Interrupted Life:
> The Diaries of Etty Hillesum,
> 1941-1943

In the face of horrific human suffering, we are seekers of meaning. Our hunger for meaning in the face of the realities of life is overwhelming.

Now this is exactly where notions of God, religion, and psychotherapy come into the picture because they, too, seek to penetrate the mystery of life, to provide us with understanding, perhaps some sense of control and alleviation, perhaps even escape.

Don't you find it interesting, Elise, that when you and I get together and have an opportunity for a long conversation, the subjects of God, religion, personal growth, and therapy come up? I find it very interesting. Since you are a P.K. (preacher's kid), perhaps it should be expected, but I think it's much more than that. Our conversations do not have the ring of "shoptalk." There is a deeper urgency and necessity in them. I love our dialogues, and I look forward to them. I especially love that you ask the right questions. It's clear that you have a deep sense that there is something profound and mysterious to life—something more, something transcendent, something that you call "God." It's also clear that traditional images and descriptions of God simply do not work for you. Sometimes you call these images sexist, sometimes patriarchal. You've said it doesn't make any sense to think about God as an old male being sitting up on

> *I, who live by words,*
> *am wordless when I try*
> *my words in prayer.*
> *All language turns*
> *To silence.*
> *Prayer will take my*
> *words and then*
> *Reveal their emptiness.*
> *The stilled voice learns*
> *To hold its peace, to*
> *listen with the heart*
> *To silence that is joy,*
> *is adoration.*
>
> *The Weather of the Heart*

the clouds somewhere running the show. Yet, you don't stop questioning or looking or searching.

Like you, Elise, I was taught that God is an ancient male being who lives or inhabits space "up in the sky," an ancient being who is perfect in every way, complete in his being, finished, done, without needs, all wise, all good, all powerful, and in no way essentially connected to creation. This God is objective, external, and conceptual. He is comprehended and communicated with only by means of the rational, logical, and philosophical dimensions of human inquiry. He is like a very good headmaster of a boy's private preparatory school. We can never have a direct personal, mutual experience of him or with him.

In fact, just about everything that I was told was "real" and constituted reality is, I have discovered, not how it is. Reality is both much more and much less than I was taught. The experience of reality is both much more wonderful and mysterious and much more gruesome and awful than either you or I were led to believe.

Likewise, Elise, you seem very clear that the religiosity and self-righteous piety of most churches feel hypocritical and offensive. You have also observed, contrary to popular belief, that those who are religious or good, who believe in God, who pray or go to church, are offered no special break from life. You know that there is, in fact, no protection from the realities of living, and that God doesn't somehow miraculously reach into life and protect, save, or deliver anybody from those harsh realities.

You have a very good shit-detector! I am glad of that and proud of you for it. You have the courage to see deeply and to raise ever more insightful and demanding questions—the important questions. You have a right to have an understanding of life; you have a right to a life that does not require you to go brain dead or deny the reality of your own experience. If we are going to talk about God, we have to talk about God in a way that does not violate our intelligence, our perceptions, our senses, or our experience. So you're asking the right questions.

I can tell from the way you ask the questions that your interest in God is not particularly academic. It seems to come out of both your need to make sense of your life and your intuitive awareness that there is something more about life than meets the eye. I also know that you have been and still are working hard in therapy, that the therapy brings clarity and solution to some things while inviting you to ask ever more penetrating and deeper questions. So, I sense in you that the therapeutic process and the dialogue about God are all part and parcel of the same process.

Dear Elise,

I KNOW IMMEDIATELY when I'm listening to someone other than you, be it a therapist, a clergy
person, a theologian, or anyone else, whether
or not his or her perceptions about reality are based on
an *experience of* God or on thoughts, beliefs, and concepts *about* God. For me, this is a crucial difference. On
the one hand is an embodied experience of God (that is,
reality) and on the other hand is a conceptual fantasy or
idealization of God: a difference, we might say, that
makes all the difference.

On the one hand, the *concept* of God is based on ideas,
"right thoughts," dogma, and other people's experience.
It is, therefore, in no way necessarily connected with the
experience of being alive, and may be nothing more than
a gratifying and comforting hypothesis. On the other
hand, the *knowing* of God in experience is rooted in and
emanates from the sensate experience of life itself. It
knows and trusts that life and one's own experience of
life are utterly revelatory of God. The knowing of God
in this mode honors the experience and honors the
human being in the human body as the receptor and
location of experience—and thus of divine revelation.
These two ways of talking about God are not very
compatible. They lead to vastly different notions about
the nature of human life, the nature of the universe and
our part in it, and the way we respond to one another
and to both the horrific and joyful experiences of being
alive.

What I want you to know, Elise, is that all around me, people I deal with both personally and professionally are asking and wrestling with the same questions. Whether they start from a therapeutic or a religious setting, they still come to a place where they want a way of knowing the world and themselves which feeds their spiritual hunger and does not demand them to make self-diminishing and self-betraying compromises, a way that does not demand they violate their intelligence or the truth of their experience. Sometimes some of us here in Maine retreat together for weekend workshops where we experience immense joy and relief in finding other like-minded people who are searching, yearning, longing, questioning, struggling. I would love to know that you have a community of people like that too.

I think we are all called to examine our lives, both individually and collectively, as honestly as possible. If our religious, philosophical, or psychological understandings of life requires us to be anything less than honest or truthful, the results can only be fraudulent. Even though the experience of being alive can be more than gruesome, at the same time, I believe it is the experience of reality itself which brings us to the presence of God. If we were to stay faithful to and ruthlessly honest about our experience with reality, I believe that is where we will find God.

I have many memories of childhood experiences that made it utterly clear to me that life was not as I was told, but rather filled with the very wonderful, very powerful, very mysterious presence—memories I would like to share with you.

My First Sacred Experience
My First Sexual Experience

○○○○○○○○○○○○○○○

HEN I WAS A LITTLE BOY, a very little boy, my father and I took baths together. The tub would have two or three inches of warm water in it and lots of little floating toys. I can well remember the warmth of the water, the slipperiness of the soap, the feel and smell of my father's body, and the size of his arms and hands as he would pick me up and place me on his lap next to his chest, the touching of our skin. Everything was unhurried and playful.

We played games, and one of my father's favorites was "hide an object." He could make a marble or a coin or one of the small floating toys disappear and reappear at will. The object would disappear and somehow emerge from my ear, from under my knee, or from between his toes. It was wonderful, miraculous, and delightful!

I remember one evening, while in the tub with my father, I became aware of his penis, how big it was, how

> In the humanity
> which is begotten today
> the Word prolongs
> the unending act
> of God's own birth;
> and by virtue
> of God's immersion
> in the world's womb,
> the great waters
> of the kingdom
> of matter have,
> without even a ripple,
> been imbued with life.
> The Immense host
> which is the universe
> is made Flesh.
>
> ———
> *Meditations With*
> *Teilhard de Chardin*

awesome, how fascinating. Instinctually, I knew that while I was drawn to stare at it, I was forbidden to touch it—or even look at it. There was something absolutely taboo about that. So, I began to sneak peaks and glances at this organ of tremendous mystery and compelling fascination.

Then he caught me looking—and I thought I would die. But he said with a smile, "You can look all you want," and I did. And he hugged me.

Body Knowing

ooooooooooooooo

I know you in my body.
>My body knows you.
My body has always known you.
>>The first few years, I didn't know
>>that it was you
>>that my body was knowing,
>>but you have never not been there.

I know the way I know you
is not the way
I was told I would know you.
>>You are not a thought
>>or a concept or a belief,
>>or even an emotion, or an insight,
>>and my body knows you.

I can touch those parts of my body
which know you best
>>in which you seem to dwell.
I can even give names
to some of the qualities
of the experience
>>of knowing you in my body,
>>and because I know you in my body,
>>there is no possible denying of knowing you.

My eyes are your eyes;
and so when I look at myself,
when I reflect upon myself,
when I consider myself,
it is at the same time
that you are seeing me.*

*All Canticles are the author's original work.

The Reality of Imagination

ooooooooooooooo

WHEN I WAS TEN YEARS OLD, my youngest
brother, Duncan, was four. He is one of
God's creatures I dearly,
dearly love; he was filled with imagination at birth.

One day, Duncan, my mother,
and I went to the Dedham Mill. My
mother loved to sew and was always
going to the mill to buy fabric. The
mill was an incredibly cavernous
building filled with bolts and bolts
and bolts of different kinds of mate-
rials.

In we went. The manager knew
my mother well, was glad to see us,
and heartily welcomed us. After
Mother selected what she needed and
we were headed for the car, Duncan
said, "Mummy, I lost my duck!"

Duncan had an imaginary pet
duck that went with him everywhere—everywhere. There was no
consoling him. It wasn't about "Oh,
we'll get a new duck" or "It'll come
home" or whatever. No, we all knew what was coming
next: my worst nightmare was coming true.

> *For this Law which I
> am laying down for you
> today is neither obscure
> for you nor beyond your
> reach. It is not in
> heaven, so that you
> need to wonder, "Who
> will go up to heaven for
> us and bring it down to
> us, so that we can hear
> and practise it?" Nor
> is it beyond the seas,
> so that you need to
> wonder, "Who will cross
> the seas for us and bring
> it back to us, so that we
> can hear and practice
> it?" No, the word is
> very near to you, it is in
> your mouth and in your
> heart for you to put
> into practice.*
>
> *Deuteronomy 30:11-14*

Realize that I was at that age at which, if your mother breathes, you're embarrassed; even having a mother was a sin.

Back into the mill we go. "Oh, hello! You wanted to buy some more material?" the manager asked with surprise. "No, Duncan lost his duck!" Well, you know, ducks are very messy creatures, and the manager was not pleased with the idea of a messy duck loose in the mill. Taking it all quite literally, he announced on the loudspeaker to all the workers in the mill that a duck was loose and it had to be found immediately.

My mother started rummaging through all kinds of material—as did everyone. Duncan scooted around doing his own search. After a grand effort, my mother said, "Oh, I found the duck!" She grabbed Duncan by one hand, stuffed the imaginary duck under her arm, and out she went saying good-bye to the manager; I trembled along behind. When we were outside, my brother said, "Mummy, it's the wrong duck! That's not my duck!" So— in we went again until he and he alone finally found his duck.

I'll never forget that. Not only was it mortifying but Duncan so ferociously hung on to a perception of truth for him that was not of this world, that we couldn't prove, but which was nonetheless real. He ferociously hung on to that reality, a reality that was beyond "normal reality."

The Cat Lover

ooooooooooooooo

WHEN I WAS YOUNG, my bedroom window looked over Marsh Street. I could clearly see 9 Marsh Street, a wonderful old, white, stately New England home with many porches. Miss Humphreys, a mysterious and ancient woman, lived at 9 Marsh Street. On rare occasions, Miss Humphreys actually came out of her house, and one could catch a glimpse of her. She was so mysterious that we never dared knock on her door at Halloween. For years, she lived by herself in that beautiful home.

From that same bedroom window, I could see 11 Marsh Street as well, where Dr. Andrews and his family lived. Dr. Andrews was a well-known and highly respected Boston surgeon, a contemporary of my parents, and a very intelligent and warm man.

On the other side of Miss Humphreys' house, separated by a driveway, were the Lathrops, a couple with children my age.

This view of three houses afforded me many hours of nighttime pleasure and entertainment and wonder.

Dr. Andrews was a ham radio operator. He had quite an array of radios and equipment in his basement. In the wee hours of the night and early morning, he loved to sit and experiment with his radios, which often emitted loud noises and strange screeches.

Now Miss Humphreys was an ardent cat lover and

the self-appointed chief antivivisectionist of Dedham, Massachusetts. Once or twice a month, in the middle of the night, the police, red lights flashing, would arrive at Dr. Andrews' home to investigate the complaint that Miss Humphreys had lodged: "I can hear the doctor next door cutting up cats."

Initially, Dr. Andrews saw some humor in this, but it wasn't long before the humor began to run a little dry. Being a Boston surgeon of some repute and having become accustomed to not being messed with, his ever increasing loudness and anger at the Dedham police became part of these late-night entertainments. All manner of effort was made by both the police and Dr. Andrews to explain to Miss Humphreys what was really going on. I believe that she was actually taken to see the radios, all to no avail. The cats were being cut up and cut up and cut up!

Meanwhile, all was not quiet at the Lathrops' either. Mr. Lathrop loved new equipment, toys, and gadgets. Naturally, the Lathrops were the first family to purchase an electric clothes dryer. As the fates would have it, the dryer was vented on the side of the house that faced Miss Humphreys' home. Every time that dryer was used, and the venting produced visible condensation of steam, often in the evening or late at night, the Dedham Fire Department was summoned. Again, all manner of effort and reason was employed to educate Miss Humphreys into the realities of the situation. Again, to no avail.

And so, for what seemed a very long time, the view from my window was this incredibly wonderful ongoing entertainment of police, fire department, and the consternation of two up-standing grown men of Dedham. Again, I knew that there were wondrous forces loose in the world impervious to all the muscular controls of reason and order and wealth and upper-class propriety.

The Baby Fish

ooooooooooooooo

MR. WRIGHT lived next door. He was an old man, a widower, with close-cut, pure white hair, a gentleman, a lifelong resident of Dedham. He had lived in his home for well over forty years.

Every Sunday, after services at the nearby Episcopal church, Mr. Wright would accept my parents' standing invitation to join them for noontime liquid refreshments. Both my parents were quite liberal on the intake of liquid refreshments, and Mr. Wright loved his bourbon. Mr. Wright's visits were enjoyable for a small boy. They brought an air of warmth, genteelness, and conviviality.

As Mr. Wright grew older, his love of liquid refreshments did not diminish, but his control over his bladder did. Just before his arrival each Sunday, my mother would very discreetly spread newspapers over the portion of the sofa where he always sat. In fact, to be honest, Mr. Wright's intake of alcohol had become a matter of concern to those who cared about him, my parents included. But no one knew how to voice that concern in a way that would not hurt his feelings. It was a dilemma.

My parents kept two ten-gallon aquariums of tropical fish in the living room, and on one particular Sunday, my mother decided that it was time to clean the tanks. Both contained a particular species (guppies, I believe) that had more than faithfully followed the biblical commandment to be fruitful and multiply; both tanks were teeming with newborn guppies. My mother's solution was to empty the contents of both tanks down the toilet and give them the flush. She put the empty tanks back just in time to spread the newspapers for the imminent arrival of Mr. Wright.

Midway into the noonday festivities, our wonderful, elderly friend and neighbor, realizing that it was time to make a trip to the bathroom, unsteadily rose from the sofa and headed in that direction. We had seen him do this a hundred times. It was a regular part of the postchurch Episcopal liturgy. A few brief moments elapsed, whereupon we heard a bloodcurdling scream, the bathroom door flew open, and out came Mr. Wright moving at a speed I had never before seen. Fully exposed, he proclaimed at the top of his lungs that he would never touch another drop of alcohol as long as he lived!

My parents helped him properly attire himself, settled him back on the couch, and fetched him a glass of water. When asked what it was that happened, he remained mute, staring straight ahead. My father discreetly went to the bathroom hoping to find a clue to the cause of Mr. Wright's sudden conversion to sobriety. He returned a few moments later with a large smile on his face, saying not a word.

Later, we were told that while most of the baby guppies had been flushed down the toilet, many had not. Evidently, they had gathered around the ring of the toilet bowl, and when our dear friend Mr. Wright began to relieve himself, the guppies were disturbed and came rushing to the center of the bowl. It would have appeared to Mr. Wright, without a doubt, that these tiny swimming, wriggling creatures had sprung forth from his loins.

Mr. Wright never did take another drink!

For me, this was simply more evidence of the mystery of reality.

Camping

○○○○○○○○○○○○○○○○

THE HIGHLIGHT OF summer camp was the week-long canoe trip. Those of us in the eleven-year-olds' cabin would spend all summer talking about it and training and preparing for this big event. One of the huge lakes in Maine would be the site of the adventure. Each day, we would paddle, make lunch, swim; and then at night, find an island suitable for overnight habitation.

On this particular trip, we did not use tents. Instead, we were given jungle hammocks which, when properly tied between two trees, are actually cooler and far more comfortable than any canvas pup tent.

That afternoon, we came easily to shore on a new island, found our campsite, collected the wood, started the fire, made supper, sang our songs, cleaned up, and retired to our own jungle hammock that we had securely fastened between two trees. It was a lovely evening.

By the middle of the night, however, things changed. An incredibly ferocious and vicious lake thunderstorm came up; it awakened me. The world around me was black, windy, rainy; the sounds and sights of thunder and lightning were close by and approaching. I lay there quietly, motionless, hardly breathing, wondering if the other kids and the two counselors were awake in their own jungle hammocks.

The lightning flashes illuminated the blackness, and

although I felt scared and fascinated, I felt safe; my two trees did not seem to be swaying in the wind.

The storm moved closer; I knew I was in trouble when I tried to breathe and couldn't fill my lungs. The air had taken on a strange electric smell. Suddenly, one of the trees to which my jungle hammock was tied was struck by lightning. It was not a flash of light or a crackling sound; it was a brightness that obliterated all color and all sight, a sound that blew all sound out of the air, and a power that burnt all the oxygen away. In my terror, I gasped for air and gasped for breath; there was none to be had.

The tree fell over and away, just above the point where my hammock was tied. I was safe and could breathe again. I lay motionless. No one came. I thought they might, but they didn't. I lay there motionless finally breathing again, knowing that I had felt a terror never before felt, but more importantly, knowing that what I had experienced was so magnificent and so important that it would change my life forever. A warming gladness came over my body. It was well worth being terrified.

God

Last week the waves were up
                    way up
A hard storm had worked its way along the
                    coast
                The tide was coming in.
First at Perkins Cove a small boy—then
an hour later
at Bald Head Cliff
a young girl and her father
                    were
Suddenly sucked away, digested by the sea.

They had come to see the majesty of waves
                to taste the salt
                        to feel the wind
                            to bathe in spray
                                to hear the crashes

Over the slippery rocks
Drawn closer and closer
What called them, killed them…effortlessly

Forty years ago, I slid and slipped
                on those very same rocks
                many times

called by the same grandeur

I lived, they didn't
Would I do it again?? No doubt
There are some risks not only worth it
but also necessary.

November 9, 1988

My Father's Voice

She Knew Me

ooooooooooooooo

WHEN YOU ARE IN the fifth grade, people in the sixth grade are gods. When I was in the fifth grade, chief among the divinities of the sixth grade was a goddess named Lisa. She was the essence of feminine loveliness, intelligence, leadership, poise, grace, and fun—certainly no less than Aphrodite herself. Everyone in the school agreed to the wonders of this young woman.

I knew lots about Lisa because I watched her a lot—but she didn't know my name. Why would she? Me, a mere prepubescent mortal. Sixth-graders, and especially Lisa, had no need of fifth-graders. I knew that to be true because, after all, I did not know the names of anyone in the fourth grade. That's just how it was!

This school had a hill. We called it the Big Hill, and big, indeed it was. In the winter, it made a superb toboggan and sledding run. One cold February afternoon, I was standing at the top of the hill, watching, won-

> *"Suddenly I understood,"* Jung writes, *"that God was, for me at least, one of the most certain and immediate of experiences."*
>
> The Illness That We Are

dering, nothing particular on my mind—and suddenly, there she was in front of me, right in front of me, directly in front of me, looking me squarely in the eye. Instantly, I began to have trouble breathing. She was standing there holding her toboggan—and she spoke:

"Michael," *oh my God, she knows my name,* "do you want to go down the hill with me on my toboggan?" Those words—that invitation was utterly inconceivable. *This is a joke* —but it wasn't. Worse than being a joke, it was real. She meant it. She chose me. She chose me from among all the other students!

I had more trouble breathing, lightheadedness set in, and I couldn't speak, not a word. I just looked at her, and again, she spoke. "Michael, get on the toboggan behind me and go down the hill with me." She was inviting me to share her toboggan with her, put my arms around her, and hold onto her, to touch her. I couldn't speak, not a word. Death would have been just fine.

Finally, in exasperation, she, the goddess, threw up her hands and chose someone else, another young man, who had no trouble breathing and speaking at all—and down the hill they went, together. Again, death would have been fine. It was my first experience of knowing what it was like to have God need something from me.

Terrifying Knowing

○○○○○○○○○○○○○○○

I hear you...I hear you.
> I hear you in my chest,
> in my heart,
> and behind and in my eyes.
I hear you in my jaw, in my throat,
and in my shoulders,
and in my groin.
> I hear you in my belly.
Mostly, I hear you in my chest.

> Because I hear you, I know you.
I know you, and it is true
that you knew me
in my mother's womb.
> I know you, and it is true
> that you are closer to me
> than I am to myself.
And because I hear you and know you,
I am more and more
in spite of myself
coming to love you
> with all my heart,
> and with all my soul,
> and with all my mind.

All my life, I have felt
a huge well-spring of love for you
at the center of my being.
>	That fact is the most terrifying fact of my life.

I know you, and now
I am able to allow
that well-spring.
>	Because I hear you and I know you,
>	I also know what you are
>	and what you are *not* saying.

Parking in Portland
After a Severe Snowstorm

◦◦◦◦◦◦◦◦◦◦◦◦◦◦◦◦

P ARKING IN PORTLAND after a severe snowstorm is always difficult, but after some effort and a little luck, I managed to wrestle my car into a metered space somewhere near the center of the city. I opened the door, climbing out and over the snowbanks. I intended to put money in the meter, but the snow was plowed so high, I couldn't find it.

As I began to walk away, I noticed one of Portland's most disheveled bag ladies shuffling her way toward me. It was clear that we were going to encounter each other. I was not in a good mood and was hoping to avoid the whole thing, but it had to happen. Perhaps I could keep it to a brief nod or a glance.

As we approached each other, the bag lady maneuvered herself directly into my path, looked at me squarely in the eye, and said in the voice of a crone, "Do you belong to that car?" "Yes," I responded hesitantly. "Are you Friar Tuck?" I said, "That's what my license plate says!"

With a twinkle in her eye, she began to move her feet in something close to a dance. She drew closer and said, "You have made my day! You look just the way I imagined you would look! I knew you were Friar Tuck!" Her delight transformed her.

Just as we were about to depart from each other, my imagination sparkled up, and I found myself saying to her, "Well, if I am Friar Tuck, who are you?" This decrepit, ancient, filthy, crone of a being winked at me and said, "I'm Maid Marion, but don't tell anybody!" And with that, she resumed her shuffle down the street.

Letter From John

ooooooooooooooo

O NE NIGHT, FINALLY, I stopped everything, prayed, meditated, and looked and listened to the fears that were disturbing me. I didn't come to any great conclusions or solutions about the fears, I only saw them all and accepted them. I believe that God is the essence of all reality, *and the more I can accept and see and feel reality, the more I know God.* Suddenly, that night, I realized that this process of accepting, seeing, and feeling reality—the process of enlightenment—is what really matters. This is the important stuff in life.

The next day, while listening to a friend's sister tell me about her experience raising two small children alone while her husband was away for many months, I felt a certain empowerment. I felt like my listening—just listening—helped her. My listening enabled her enlightenment.

So, there you are; I saw the critical importance of enlightenment, and I saw my own special ability to enable enlightenment in others by listening/talking—all this in one weekend!

> *The self is shattered,*
> *all words torn apart*
> *In this strange patterned*
> *time of contemplation*
> *That, in time, breaks*
> *time, breaks words,*
> *breaks me,*
> *And then, in silence,*
> *leaves me healed*
> *and mended.*
> *I leave, returned to*
> *language, for I see*
> *Through words, even*
> *when all words are*
> *ended. I, who live*
> *by words,*
> *am wordless when*
> *I turn me to the Word*
> *to pray. Amen.*
>
> *The Weather of the Heart*

Nana

oooooooooooooooo

I WAS BLESSED. I had wonderful grandparents. All four of them were distinctly chiseled people of character. They couldn't have been more different from one another except they shared the inner conviction about being nobody else but themselves. Each, in his or her own way, went about that with gusto. I was blessed not only with the who of each of them, but also—and perhaps more powerfully—with their inner conviction of the essential rightness of being that who and nobody else, a double blessing.

My father's mother—we called her "Nana"—came from Wyle and Smith stock of the Pennsylvania Dutch country of Lancaster County. She loved her martinis and her sherry. She loved the Red Sox. She loved bridge. She loved her diamonds. She loved quick-wittedness and humor and ideas. Every Friday, Nana would walk to the bank and turn in all her change and green money for new change and new bills. She insisted upon clean, fresh money. At Christmas, we often received rolls of dimes and quarters from her, and we knew that they would be gleaming freshly minted. She had a wonderful energy in her eyes; they were always twinkling. She also did not suffer fools gladly.

People were sometimes afraid of Nana, but throughout my childhood, I was never afraid of her. I found her intriguing, and I loved her!

Nana was diagnosed with terminal cancer while I was in my middle year of seminary. When I went to visit her in the hospital, I knew that it would be the last time we would ever talk.

I was afraid, not of Nana so much but of the situation. Because I was a seminarian and training to be a priest, I thought I was supposed to know what I was supposed to say, but I had never said good-bye to a dying person before. The fear was of my own feelings, of saying something inappropriate, of not knowing what to say, of maybe not saying enough, and of knowing that Nana and I had never had a personal intimate conversation before.

Nana knew I was coming to visit. She knew the reason for the visit, and she looked her best. When I entered her hospital room, she invited me to have a seat. Very quickly, I ran out of conversation. I was finished with pleasantries, and it was obvious that I was at a loss for words and very nervous.

She blessed me again. She said, "Michael, I know you have never done this before, and I have never died before. So neither of us knows how to do this, or what we are supposed to do." She paused and said, "You have been a wonderful grandson. You have made

> *Over every living thing which is to spring up, and to grow, to flower, to ripen during his day, say again the words: This is my Body. And over every death-force which awaits in readiness to corrode, to wither, to cut down, speak again your commanding words which express the supreme mystery of faith: This is my Blood.*
>
> ———
> *Meditations With Teilhard de Chardin*

me very proud, and you have made your father very proud!"

She had freed me from my fear, and I was able to tell her what a very wonderful grandmother she had been and how much I loved her. We were able to say good-bye.

She was a classy woman. She did not have much use for the foolishness of organized religion, and…she was so full of grace.

ooooooooooooooo

My dreams always seemed just so much fodder
for my intellectual ability to chew upon.
My intellect was always so far ahead of my numbed
feelings which needed to be stirred into life.
But now, at long last, my feelings are waking up the
numbed deadness of my body...I now realize that,
ultimately, I cannot release my creativity
until my body is freed. As Alice Miller writes:
"The truth about our childhood is stored up
in our body, and although we can repress it,
we can never alter it. Our intellect can be deceived,
our feelings manipulated, our perceptions confused
and our bodies tricked with medication.
But someday the body will present its bill,
for it is as incorruptible as a child who,
still whole in spirit, will accept no compromises
or excuses, and it will not stop tormenting us
until we stop evading the truth."

Leaving My Father's House:
The Journey to Conscious Femininity

II

ooooooooooooooo

The Denial
of Reality

ooooooooooooooo

Dear Elise,

CKNOWLEDGING THAT LIFE is very, very hard, it is more than understandable that since our beginnings, we human beings have attempted to devise strategies, philosophies, religions, and psychologies that help us with life's hardness. Perhaps the experience can be made easier, more bearable. So, our history as a species is marked by a whole ongoing series of alternative versions of life, what might be called "idealized fabricated realities," invented versions of life that are seen as superior, as solutions, as escapes, as antidotes, as shields. Some people call these addictions; others call them immortality projects. I like "idealized fabricated realities," myself.

In the end, of course, they all fail us and simply worsen the pain and the terror and the disappointment because we feel so disillusioned and betrayed. So, while the construction of these fabricated realities is understandable, the effort must also be seen as dangerous, spirit draining, and soul eviscerating. The bigger the fabrication, of course, the harder the crash and the deeper the spiritual hunger.

> *This is not to say that Christianity is finished. I am, on the contrary, convinced that it is not Christianity, but our conception and our interpretation of it that has become antiquated in the face of the present world situation. The Christian symbol is a living thing that carries in itself the seeds of further development. It can go on developing; it only depends on us, whether we can make up our minds to meditate again, and more thoroughly, on the Christian premise.*
>
> *The Undiscovered Self*

Whenever a fabricated reality is constructed, life itself becomes the enemy and the experience of reality becomes the thing we are trying to avoid, escape from, alter, or find a superior substitute for.

In life the experience of reality is the bringer of God, then when we fabricate an alternative reality and turn life into the enemy, God becomes the enemy. Joseph Campbell said that organized religion is man's invention to protect himself from ever having a direct encounter with the living God.

Religion and psychotherapy are full of fabricated realities, Elise, some of which I'd like to describe.

Dear Elise,

I HAVE BEEN WANTING to share with you some of my perceptions about a few of these fabricated realities which may be popular, but are nonetheless pseudocomforting illusions. Perhaps this would be a good way for me to let you know how some of the traditional and current beliefs ask me to violate my intelligence, my instincts, my experience, or all three. I imagine that you and I would find ourselves with many common thoughts.

It is not uncommon to hear people asking God in prayer to "let" their car pass the annual state safety inspection or petitioning God to "tell" them when to take their exams and how to answer the questions...or maybe even asking God or Jesus to "make" a business deal succeed. I have always been offended by this mode of praying because it assumes that the God of the universe, of the whole cosmos, the creator of everything that is and isn't, is concerned with and can be manipulated into being a positive active player in the minute details of a person's life, a housebroken, domesticated pet. There is something about this kind of praying that seems, at least to me, arrogant, narcissistic, and egocentric.

There are, of course, other and perhaps more sophisticated variations of this theme. For instance, the notion that God's singular purpose in the universe is to save me from my own sinfulness; if I should happen to repent enough and pray enough, God will do something for me so that I can feel better about myself. Again, the "I" is most important, and again, there is the assumption that God exists to relieve me of my guilty perceptions of not being a good enough person. In fact, it is a narcissistic humility because it assumes that the more fervently we confess to being a totally abject sinner, the more God will do what we want: favor us. Often this position is cloaked with a great deal of humility.

It is also commonly held that to be involved with God is about good and bad, about morality. This perception sees God as being primarily involved in good and bad, that is, my perception, your perception, our perception of good and bad. (But not "theirs." Please note that these perceptions of morality change radically from person to person and culture to culture.) This is a very shallow reading of Scripture and an equally shallow understanding of human nature. Yet, it conveniently supports our need to have our personal, invented view of reality reinforced.

Another manifestation or symptom of the narcissism or arrogance of much of religion is the inherent moral superiority that an in-group of believers rewards itself with. "God is on our side." "We are the chosen people." "People who aren't like us and don't see reality the way we do are inferior and bad, and all manner of horrible and vicious behavior toward

> *For these differing reasons Jung charged the major Western Christian traditions with blocking rather than enabling the access of their followers to the life they claim to mediate. In this climate conceptions of faith are divorced from any experiential basis in humanity's awareness of itself, and become dehumanizing substitutes for the life-giving experience of the unconscious which the symbols express.*
>
> *The Illness That We Are*

'them' is justified in the name of God." This attitude is really pernicious. God becomes very useful, serving and blessing the needs and desires and aggressions of the "true believer" either in a gross and obvious manner or sometimes in a more subtle and sophisticated manner.

There is a story about how American soldiers in the First World War were shocked when they came across the bodies of dead German soldiers and discovered that *Gott mit uns* (God with us) was written on the Germans' belt buckles. The Americans were convinced, of course, that they were fighting in God's holy cause, and that God was on *their* side. After all, God couldn't possibly be pro-American and pro-German at the same time!

There is a notion that if people, through some form of piety, can win God to their side, then God will grant "victory" to them or their side or their cause. Then, of course, if victory—or whatever it is—is not forthcoming, it must mean that the petitioners have not been pious enough. This is simply manipulative magic.

This narcissism and egocentricity easily spreads from one person into groups—small groups, large groups, particular churches, cults, nations, races, even the whole human species. We often assume that God is more interested in human beings than in the rest of creation, that we are, therefore, superior to

Thus the full price of the revitalization and broadening of the human spirit attached to Jung's challenging understanding of the human psyche and its religious propensities may ultimately prove to be too high for an individual of a community clinging to its no doubt God-given, but partial, revelation as final, unique and all-encompassing.

The Illness That We Are

other animals; we assume, I am certain, that the survival of the human species in the universe is a key concern of God. The coming of God's kingdom is thought to depend on the survival of the human species. Whole theologies and belief structures are built around these assumptions, which I think are, in fact, transparently self-serving and convenient and, therefore, at the very least, highly suspect, and at worst give license to an incredibly arrogant, entitled, and socially dangerous attitude toward the rest of creation.

I must admit that on rare occasions there have been miraculous recoveries from incurable situations, and rescues from desperate straights, but these things happen to the just and the unjust alike, the pious and the pagans, the believers and the nonbelievers. Far, far more often, people are struck down and die with terminal illnesses; natural and man-made tragedies wreak unabated destruction. People's lives fail and come to naught. They crash and burn regardless of how mentally healthy they are, how morally perfect they are, or how enlightened they are. There simply is no hiding from suffering and evil (one's own and others') and death.

These and other traditional ways of understanding God seem to me to require a gross denial of the facts and realities of our lives, and must, therefore, inevitably leave us hungry. They rob us of spiritual food and are ultimately dangerous.

Dear Elise,

HAVE YOU EVER NOTICED how a group or a cause or a movement that starts out proclaiming or being identified with something positive inevitably moves in the direction of becoming over-identified with the good, the true, and the positive? Do you remember how President Reagan, in his need to buttress the goodness of the United States, began referring to the Soviet Union only in terms of super bad: "the evil empire"?

This dynamic of moving from positive to the super one-sided positive, and thus the denial and disidentification from anything "negative," is most prevalent in religion and psychology. Not only is the negative denied and disidentified with but it becomes projected onto any other group or institution that is markedly different or perhaps simply handy.

The most significant religious movement in the twentieth century has been the rise of Nazi Germany. The predominant historical fact of that fanatic religious movement was the projection of the negative (or some call it the shadow) onto anyone of Jewish heritage. This

> *The most depressing thing of all is that the mental horizon of all the people I work with is so narrow. They don't even suffer deep down. They just hate and blind themselves to their own pettiness, the intrigue; they are still ambitious to get on; it is all a great big, dirty mess and there are moments when I would like to lay my head down on my typewriter and say in despair, "I can't go on like this."*
>
> *An Interrupted Life: The Diaries of Etty Hillesum, 1941–1943*

projection was so ferocious and so complete that it justified the slaughter and extermination of seven million people over a six-year period. Ethnic cleansing in our own times, while on a smaller scale, is an identical dynamic; it is done all in the name of God. There are large numbers of white Americans who call themselves Christians and dress in robes and burn crosses and threaten, intimidate, violate, and lynch Blacks—in the name of God's goodness.

Whenever God is conceived as the highest good, and only the highest good—the largest positive as pure love— then those who worship and follow God most naturally assume that they are on the side of, aligned with, in service of, and protected by that which is the highest good. They are, therefore, cleansed of the darkness that inhabits all of us, and are finally commended and given license to eliminate those upon whom they project their own denied darkness. As long as God remains only good and the highest good, we will be forever plagued by this hideous, possibly fatal, dynamic.

It is, indeed, emotionally comfortable and convenient to imagine God as all-good, all-powerful, and all-loving; but when we do that, we set in motion this terrible dynamic of denial and the projection on others of everything that isn't good and loving.

In psychology and counseling, Elise, the same dynamic is present. The words change, of course; in the place of all-good, all-loving, and all-powerful are words like cure, wholeness, health, happiness, empowerment, safety, and comfort. The opposites of these positive virtues are seen as negative: illness, confusion, failure, dependence, depression, and brokenness. We counselors often find our-selves talking with derision and contempt about other people whose lives are broken and full of suffering. If, after years of therapy, a client hasn't changed his or her situation or life very much, and the stress remains at the same level, guilt and blame are often passed out by both the client and the therapist. It is a "failure" and a "sin" not to "get better." People who are unschooled or unaware of psychological lan-guage, understanding, and insights are perceived often as unsophisti-cated, naive, ignorant, and incapable of intelligent, insightful, empathetic thoughts, feelings, and behaviors. The shadow of psychology and therapy is projected with almost as much regularity and vehe-mence as is the shadow of religion.

> *What is hidden beneath the literal meaning is not merely another and more hidden meaning; it is also a new and totally different reality....It is the divine life itself.*
>
> *Bread in the Wilderness*

The wonderful truth about our own human experi-ence of ourselves is that we are incredibly complex and mysterious mixtures of opposites—good and evil, health and illness, wholeness and brokenness, light and dark-ness, and many more. The opposites are inextricably bound together, and it is the energy and tension between the opposites that provide the necessary fuel to keep the whole human psychology and spiritual enterprise running.

Dear Elise,

FOR TWENTY-FIVE YEARS, I have listened to people tell me the stories of their lives, particularly the hard, wounded, broken, or troubled chapters of those stories. And for twenty-five years, I have listened to other pastoral counselors and therapists talk about what they—we—do, what helps and what hinders, how to understand pain and its relief, woundedness and its healing. Therapy itself, going to therapy, being a therapist, has become a twentieth-century phenomenon.

Granted, there are some aspects of that which seem to be full of validity and integrity. But there is a good deal about it that bothers me and disturbs me in ways that are similar to how I am bothered and disturbed by traditional religion. The words and labels in therapy and religion are different, but I think the actual dynamics are often the same. While religion speaks of "sin" and "redemption," therapy speaks about "sickness" and "wholeness."

It seems to me that therapy assumes that there is a cure or even a superior substitute for a great sickness, a great sickness called "life," and that this or that mode of therapy or program or regimen or drug or jargon or rhetoric, if adhered to strenuously, will bring cure and wholeness for a wide variety of life's ailments—even life itself.

One of therapy's oversimplified solutions to the difficulties of human living is the so-called "developmental model." The notion is that whatever is not working or is difficult for a person has its root causes somewhere in that person's past, usually in childhood. Whatever is wrong, therefore, can be located in the patient's history and, through a variety of techniques, can be "worked through." This understanding has several problems, one of which is that it understands time as only moving in one direction: from the past into the future; meaning has to be a product located in the past. Other cultures at other times and other places, noticing something wrong with a person, would never ask, "What was the trouble in your childhood? What kind of mother or father did you have?" They would not look to the past.

> *Tillich could thus have counted on Jung's support in the view that the development of Christian theology since the introduction of Aristotle through Aquinas has been one leading consistently to the loss of the inner sense of God.*
>
> The Illness That We Are

So our current psychological way of looking at the source of difficulties is highly limited and simplistic and does not take into account the complexity of human psychological and spiritual experience. Experience is denied in favor of theory.

Another drawback of this model is that it tends to invite people to see themselves as victims—victims of their history, victims of their past, victims of their circumstances, victims of their parents or families, whatever. If there is a bad outcome, it must be somebody else's fault. If I am in pain, there must be somebody to blame. The emphasis on the victim role tends to leave persons in a helpless, childlike, but overly entitled mindset. They, thus, can become overly reliant upon the healer, or even the legal system, feeling that somehow life, living itself, has dealt everyone else a good hand except for them. They grow to feel outrageously entitled.

A third drawback of our modern psychological understanding is the idealization of the child or the inner child. The presumption is that the child at birth is in some natural state of innocence and is totally equipped with all the necessary understanding tools, instincts, values, feelings, perceptions, attitudes, and so on to enjoy full, complete, meaningful, and joyful living. Then, somehow, in being raised to adulthood, the child is inhibited, wounded, broken, and deformed by the adult world. The early stages of life are seen as far more important than later stages. The purpose of therapy then becomes to release or free that inner child, to heal it back to its original state of innocence, and to set it free to live the way it was supposed to always live before it became contaminated. The illusion is that the child is innocent, good, and pure, creating, therefore, a powerful bias against maturity and complexity which, in turn, gives rise to a fierce preference for idealization and spirit over and against the depths and darkness of soul.

I could give many more examples of therapy's bias against life and therapy's notion that psychology can find the cause of, fix the blame for, and provide the cure or superior alternative for the conditions of life and living itself.

Remember this, Elise: In therapy or religion, when you hear people talk about blame or the cause or the cure, you are in the presence of an ever-enlarging pile of you-know-what!

Remember, also, that to wrap people in a cloak of innocence and purity or powerlessness and victimhood is to rob them of the potential of knowing God, of knowing soul.

Remember that when therapy talks about providing a safe place, it is using a relative term because, finally, there is no safe place; there are only places that are a little bit safer than others. We can never be made safe from the fact that we are alive.

Finally, when someone says, "The effects of child sexual abuse are lifelong," implying some special victimhood, remember that powerful effects of being born are also lifelong. To be born is to be born into, among other things, a lifelong experience of pain and loss. The deepening of awareness, something we all seek, comes at a huge price. For with each new level of awareness comes a new level of accountability and responsibility and sensitivity to the world around us.

There is no escape from life. There is no solution for life. There is nobody to blame for life. There is no cure from life, either from life's tremendous internal struggles and tensions or from its external vicissitudes and horrors. Any attempt to provide an escape, an excuse, a cause, or a solution is finally a

> *Forgive us, O Lord,*
> *we acknowledge*
> *ourselves as type*
> *of the common man,*
> *Of the men and women*
> *who shut the door*
> *and sit by the fire;*
> *Who fear the blessings*
> *of God,*
> *the loneliness*
> *of the night of God,*
> *The surrender required,*
> *the deprivation*
> *inflicted;*
> *Who fear the injustice*
> *of men less than the*
> *justice of God;*
> *Who fear the hand at*
> *the window, the fire*
> *in the thatch, the fist in*
> *the tavern, the push*
> *into the canal,*
> *Less than we fear the*
> *love of God.*
>
> Murder in the Cathedral:
> The Complete Poems and Plays,
> 1909-1950

romantic or sentimentalized—maybe even intriguing—diversion, but a diversion nonetheless. Any therapy or religion that claims otherwise is a thief who comes in the night to steal and rob us blind. Any therapy or religion that claims to offer an alternative superior to the experience of life itself is, likewise, criminal.

Dear Elise,

THE BIBLE, in its variety of content and style, is fundamentally and primarily a book about God. Particularly, it speaks of God as the Holy One who, most essentially and accurately, can be described as the One who becomes.

Becoming is the chief activity of God. "I am whom I shall be. Behold, my business is to recreate everything as new. My Word becomes Flesh. I become human." And on and on and on. Being and doing are derivative subcategories of God's becoming. The kingdom of heaven doesn't just exist, nor is it complete. It is constantly becoming. It never stops breaking in; it is never completely broken in, so it is never finished breaking in. It is always becoming, pressuring every moment to become something more.

Sarah understood herself well. She knew the biology of her own body, and she knew that she had passed beyond the years when her body could bear children. Her being and history were that of an old woman no longer capable of pregnancy, and her doing was as wife of Abraham. Sarah thought she knew herself well, but she

> Instead of considering revelation to be somehow over and done with, ending with the historical closing of the canon, a psychological perspective would understand revelation to continue in the individual dialogue between ego and unconscious. The New Testament or Covenant would cease to be a once upon a time contract whose terms are spelled out in sacred texts. Rather a genuinely new testament would be struck every time the individual was led by the Self into dialogue with it, in the interest of the Self's more conscious incarnation.
>
> The Illness That We Are

had neglected to account for the becoming of God, and thus, likewise, her own becoming.

What was Sarah's becoming? It was not to be found in her past. So when the angel tells her that she is going to conceive and bring forth a child, she, rooted in the certain historical knowledge of her past, of her physiological being, laughs.

And then, of course, her becoming comes across the bridge from the future and meets her, overwhelming, eclipsing, disregarding, contradicting her past, the history of her being and doing. She becomes a mother. God, in becoming, is simply not confined to, determined or limited by history. In fact, God overwhelms history in never before seen and unpredictable manifestations of divine newness.

The language of addiction is a premiere language and metaphor of the therapeutic and perhaps even the religious community. It is possible that history, or more particularly, a causal linear understanding of history, is the foundational addiction from which all other addictions spring. Furthermore, it is possible that both conventional religion and conventional psychotherapy, as practiced and experienced in the late twentieth century, are profoundly addicted to a causal determinative understanding of history. We believe that we are defined by the events of our past. We believe that for everything that goes wrong in our present lives there is a cause, a reason, in our past that will explain everything. We believe that if we understand our pasts well enough, we can avoid repeating the mistakes and even shape our futures more to our liking. It's as if the past were God, and in fact, we often think of God in the past tense. Our religious doctrines and practices are shaped, determined, and fixed on how it has been done in the past, and if we should try to do something new that has not been done in the past, it cannot be allowed.

Patients in therapy spend weeks and months—sometimes years—recalling and reexamining the events of their lives. Therapists take long and extensive histories. In spiritual discernment groups, we listen to people telling their stories from the past for clues and signs of how God is present in their lives. We believe that we are the products of our history, that we are determined by our history, and that our history has caused us to be who we are and, therefore, who we will be. We are addicted to this perception of reality.

It becomes, then, very important to find ways to control the future, or at least provide the illusion of control. Think of all the energy we put into that enterprise of controlling the future.

Chief among them, I believe, are those behaviors we call addictions. Take for example, alcoholism. What a truly wonderful controller of the future it is. If you are in the middle of your day and you find yourself coming up on a period of time when you are not sure what is going to happen, either around you or within you, you reach for a drink. If you start feeling a little shaky in the presence of an unknown and unpredictable future, a little alcohol will help. It's powerful; it works every time, absolutely. Once the alcohol is in your system, the same wonderful and awful emotional, physical, and spiritual process takes place. The alcohol guarantees that the future will be, at least for the next few hours, predictable, under control. Whatever damage the alcohol does, it is not as egregious as facing into the unknown and unpredictable future of divine becoming.

> *It would mean that a living theology could only arise from the theologian's experience of those powers which Jung locates in the unconscious; such theology, moreover, would be continually enlivened as the theologian sought to give ever more conscious and reflective form to his or her experience.*
>
> *This would indeed be in marked contrast to the current practice of theology, which too often is an effort to give some form of conscious validation to someone else's experience, itself considered as a piece of conscious though unlikely data.*
>
> The Illness That We Are

More effective than alcohol in providing illusions that control our future are our models of religion and therapy. Both claim to understand the nature of reality itself and provide methods and practices that assure desired and predictable outcomes. These models are not based on the experience of living, but rather on idealized fantasies of how we would like life to be.

Not only is that perception of reality addictive, it is also, from a theological point of view, idolatrous. It completely ignores and neglects the possibility that we are perhaps not products of our past, but indeed, products of our future, or more precisely, products of our becoming, products of the ongoing becoming process of God in and through each of us, a process which can, as it did in Sarah's case, totally eclipse the facts of our history and produce an outcome, a new creation, that was in no way predictable from within the events of the past. We are not human beings or human doings. That is a false duality. We are human becomings. Therapy patients remain frozen and tyrannized by their history until they are able to revision the entirety of their history from a new standpoint in the present shaped by a vision of the future. It's not so much that the facts of the history change; rather the viewpoint and the interpretation change. And what enables a change in viewpoint, in interpretation, and in perspective? The becoming of the patient in the present so that the past can be held in a new way, in a way that does not tyrannize or dominate, but in a way that contributes value to the present becoming.

Likewise in spiritual direction. The presence of God in one's history can only be understood and perceived through the viewpoint of the becoming of God in a person's life as the present is intersected by the future. What if churches were beginning to understand this? The entire two thousand years of Church history begs for revisioning through the experience of the becoming of God in the lives of people living presently. When a person or an institution is addicted to history, history dominates and has ultimate authority over the meaning of things, and hence, the ongoing becoming of God becomes subjugated, minimized, and denied.

> *For it clearly implies that God depends on human consciousness for a redemption lacking to the divine life in itself. This implication is hostile to traditional ideas of divine transcendence and self-sufficiency. It would demand radical recasting of such entral themes as the gratuity of creation and the nature of the fall since both men (Jung and Eckhart) imply that the universal truth of original sin is the sin of becoming conscious.*
>
> *A Strategy for a Loss of Faith: Jung's Proposal*

Dear Elise,

I WOULD LIKE TO GIVE an example of how a fabricated and distorted reality, no matter how alluring and wonderful it sounds, ends up causing additional anguish and grief because it has no real substance.

Today, I saw a client who has epilepsy. She has been diagnosed for a long time and is on medication that prevents her from having to suffer the seizures. But someone recently chided her about the medication saying that, after all, if she really admitted it, she would have to confess that she had given herself the epilepsy, and that if she simply reversed that decision, she would not need the medication. She was really upset, of course, because, like lots of other people, she believes that in some way all of us are consciously and willfully responsible for our entire lives. Her assumptions were that we can have the lives we choose. In fact, the lives we have are the way they are because we choose them. If we are ill, it's because we have chosen to be ill. We even choose the parents that we end up with.

My client was feeling shame and guilt and anguish because, if in fact we are in some way willfully responsible for the entirety of our lives, she had given herself epilepsy, and it was up to her to take responsibility for that choice; it was up to her to do something about it.

What a terrible and cruel hoax this so-called therapeutic insight has become. It is but another example of immense egocentricity; my ego-consciousness and your ego-consciousness are the true center of everything, are in control of everything, choose everything—that means being in control of the unconscious, of all the forces of nature, of all the dynamics and powers that are invisible, even of God. It means that when something goes wrong,

and it always will, the person must bear not only the pain and suffering of it but also the guilt and shame. It is still hard to mention cancer or mental illness or depression because we are afraid that we are going to be shamed for simply being human.

It is our humanity, our simple, deep and complex humanity, that always takes a licking in the presence of fabricated realities. They provide the illusion of temporary relief and comfort—but always at the humiliating cost of some essential and real part of our lives.

Fabricated realities: the control of God through piety or good works or humble confessions of sinfulness. Fabricated realities: the defining of God (or mental health) in a very particular way that is always to the advantage of those who do the defining. Fabricated realities: an understanding of time and history that seeks to make human life and the human spirit predictable, controllable,

However, conventional religion and conventional psychotherapy both try, consciously or unconsciously, to deny their roots in the numinous. The sense of the numinous is all but lost upon modern Christians, and in psychology the mysteries of the soul are dismissed in favor of rationalistic explanations for human behavior and problems. This sentiment was once expressed by Jung in one of his letters, in which he said: "The clinical practice of psychotherapy is a mere makeshift that does its utmost to prevent numinous experiences."

Mystical Christianity

definable, and quantifiable. Fabricated realities: regression into idealized, romanticized, and sentimentalized versions of goodness or wellness.

I could cite many more realities, and I'm sure you'd like to add some to the list yourself, Elise. They all have one thing in common: in the name of trying to protect us from the experience of reality itself—or in theological language, from an encounter with the living God—they, in fact, stand between and block us from the very thing that can bring integrity, meaning, hope, and love. The paradox is, of course, that it is life at its most horrific which also bears the fruit of the most beautiful and blessed graces.

Fabricated reality is a thief stealing the jewels out of our very hands in the name of trying to be helpful.

In Search of the Holy

ooooooooooooooo

For the Cry is not outside us, it does not come
from a great distance that we may escape it.
It sits in the center of our hearts, and cries out.
God shouts: "Burn your houses! I am coming!
Whoever has a house cannot receive me!
Burn your ideas, smash your thoughts!
Whoever has found the solution cannot find me.
I love the hungry, the restless, the vagabonds.
They are the ones who brood eternally on hunger,
on rebellion, on the endless road—on ME!
I am coming! Leave your wives, your children,
your ideas, and follow me. I am the great Vagabond.
Follow! Stride over joy and sorrow, over peace and
justice and virtue! Forward! Smash these idols,
smash them all; they cannot contain me.
Smash even yourself that I may pass."
Set fire! This is our great duty today amid
such immoral and hopeless chaos.

———

The Rock Garden

III

ooooooooooooooo

Reality as the Tension of the Opposites

ooooooooooooooo

Dear Elise,

I CAN VERY WELL REMEMBER—in fact, how could I forget—the first time I saw you wrestle with the process of becoming through the terrible struggle of opposites.

I think you were in the third grade. You had been home from school for a couple of hours when I came up from my office and found you crying in an inconsolable way. It seemed like almost forever before you would talk about your tears, about why you were so, so upset. You told the following story:

You had been walking down the hallway at school and had come upon a classmate lying on the floor. He was, I think, as you described him, the class bully, or the class jerk; nobody liked him, including you. He caused trouble for many people. In fact, he was able to make some of your classmates' lives miserable.

There he was lying on the floor. He had been fighting and somehow had been pushed down; there was a whole group of kids standing around him, taunting him, obviously delighting in his misery.

You told me that you walked up to the scene, stopped, looked at what was happening, and without thinking about it, spontaneously kicked him, maybe more than once, and then you walked away. You then told me that you found yourself, quite to your horror, to have enjoyed the experience of kicking him and relishing the memory. Finally, you said that when the teacher asked you about the incident later on that day and whether or not you had been involved or had seen anything, you simply told her a series of bold-faced lies.

You were totally horrified with your own behavior. You couldn't believe that you had spontaneously kicked the boy, enjoyed it, and then lied about it. You kept saying, "Daddy, that's not me. That's not me! That's not the person I am." And I knew, of course, that it wasn't you. You were and are a kind person, not given to hurting people or taking pleasure in people's pain. And I have always known you to be incredibly truthful. In the third grade, you were stuck in an image of yourself of being very, very good. I saw you as quite confined and restricted by that self-image, and so, in the midst of your true pain and disbelief and fear of yourself, I was secretly delighted; you were encountering the spontaneous eruption of dimensions of you that you had never consciously known. In the juxtaposition of Elise as "very good girl" on the one hand, and Elise as "nasty lying sadist" on the other hand, I wanted you to come to a freedom and a breathing space, an expansion and growth, a possibility of becoming a different and new person. I saw the situation as a wonderful

> ### Search the Darkness
>
> *Sit with your friends;*
> *don't go back to sleep.*
> *Don't sink like a fish to*
> *the bottom of the sea.*
>
> *Surge like an ocean,*
> *don't scatter yourself*
> *like a storm.*
>
> *Life's waters flow*
> *from darkness.*
> *Search the darkness,*
> *don't run from it.*
>
> *Night travelers are*
> *full of light,*
> *and you are, too;*
> *don't leave this*
> *companionship.*
>
> *Be a wakeful candle*
> *in a golden dish,*
> *don't slip into the dirt*
> *like quicksilver.*
>
> *The moon appears for*
> *night travelers,*
> *be watchful when*
> *the moon is full.*
>
> ---
>
> *Love Is a Stranger*

moment for you; in fact, as the months went on, you lightened up. Your sense of humor increased, your self-confidence grew, your ability to assert yourself and speak out for yourself deepened and expanded. You had, indeed, "become" through the bearing of the tension of your own irreconcilable opposites.

I wonder if you have ever seen that struggle and that divine process in me?

The Light of the Dark

ᴏᴏᴏᴏᴏᴏᴏᴏᴏᴏᴏᴏᴏᴏ

THE DRIVE THROUGH the foothills of the Blue Ridge Mountains back to Lexington, Virginia, was a long one. The moon was hidden. It was late at night and very dark.

I was driving the ambulance, and the captain and the first lieutenant of the volunteer rescue squad were riding with me. We were returning from a routine call that had taken us far into the outer reaches of Rockbridge County.

The three of us were talking, and the name of a new member came up. Recently, he had been voted into the squad and was in his ninety-day probation period. This new member had just informed us that he would be taking his long summer vacation during his probation period, thus, in effect, cutting his probation period by about thirty days.

Well, that certainly rubbed me the wrong way. I began, full of righteousness and eloquence, to sternly moralize about the motivation of anyone who wanted to be part of our rescue squad taking vacation during the probationary period. I went on and on, getting quite carried away with my righteousness. Then, I began to notice. I noticed that the more I talked, the quieter the captain and the first lieutenant became. I thought that they either disapproved of my opinion or didn't quite understand it. So, I went around the whole thing again with even more vehemence. Their stillness and silence became terrifying, and finally quieted me altogether.

Now you must understand, these were Rockbridge County Virginians who had never before had to deal with a Harvard, Yankee, Episcopal priest, especially one who was both a member and their chaplain. Finally, the captain, with an ever-growing smile on his face—he knew he had me—said, "Michael, you did exactly the same thing."

He might as well have struck a hammer blow to my stomach. I gasped for air; my chest tightened; I stammered, and finally had to pull the ambulance over to the side of the road because, of course, he was right. I had done the same thing. I had taken my vacation during my probation. The prophet Daniel's words to King David rang with stunning clarity through my head: "You are the man," and I was fully exposed. These two men whom I, in my academic snobbery and moral self-righteousness, had thought could never teach me a thing had just taught me one of the most important lessons of my life. I was stunned, crushed, relieved, and saved.

We are conditioned to think that a great vision will bring angelic experience, creativity, delight; it does, but its most salient effect is to constellate the shadow! The conscious hope is for angelic things, peace, love, creativity; but it is the shadow that brings the energy to live as a human being. No one can be anything but a partial being, ravaged by doubt and loneliness, unless he has close contact with his shadow.

Transformation: Understanding the Three Levels of Masculine Consciousness

The Reconciling Third

ooooooooooooooo

Bollingen, 20 August 1945.

Dear Frau Frobe,
　…There can be no resolution, only patient endurance
of the opposites which ultimately spring from your own
nature. You yourself are a conflict that rages in itself and
against itself, in order to melt its incompatible substances,
the male and the female, in the fire of suffering, and
thus create that fixed and unalterable form which is the
goal of life. Everyone goes through this mill, consciously
or unconsciously, voluntarily or forcibly. We are crucified between the opposites and delivered up to the tor-
ture until the "reconciling third" takes shape. Do not
doubt the rightness of the two sides within you, and let
whatever may happen, happen….The apparently unen-
durable conflict is proof of the rightness of your life. A
life without inner contradiction is either only half a life
or else a life in the Beyond, which is destined only for
angels. But God loves human beings more than the angels.
　With kindest regards,

Yours sincerely,
C.G. Jung

C.G. Jung Letters, Volume 1: 1906-1950

Who Died?

ooooooooooooooo

WHEN I BEGAN my three-month internship at the state mental hospital, I thought my primary purpose as a student chaplain was to bring pastoral care to some of the patients. By the time the three months had passed, I realized that the purpose of the internship had been, in fact, to test both the depths of my faith and the limits of my sanity. Three months of that was about all I could deal with!

The state hospital was so big that I was one of about twenty student chaplains. I was assigned three different East wards, mostly populated by elderly, frail, and catatonic women, women kept in subdued tranquillity with heavy doses of medication, people forgotten by the world; they never received mail or visitors. It was a place I had never thought I would find myself in because I could not possibly imagine it. A sense of impotent uselessness accompanied most of my days because I had no idea what to say or do. My Episcopal, WASP, religious tradition had not one thing to offer these people. I had come to think it must be true that this place was one of those places which surely God had abandoned.

The hospital was so big that it was divided down the middle by a large metropolitan highway. If someone became medically ill, an ambulance had to be called from the West side to transfer the person to the medical ward for appropriate medical care.

One hot summer afternoon it became eminently clear that one of the patients was having severe difficulty breathing and required immediate medical attention. The ambulance was called, arrived, and the patient was loaded onto the cot and carried from the ward out onto the sidewalk. Then a discussion that turned into an argument ensued between the ambulance driver and the head nurse of the ward. It seemed that the appropriate "ward transfer papers" had not been filled out, and the ambulance driver could not or would not load the patient into the ambulance without those papers, regardless of how serious the emergency.

The discussion turned into a heated argument. Several people stood around and watched, myself included. There seemed to be no solution. The patient lay in the sun on the cot beside the ambulance. Finally, when some truce had been established, the nurse and the driver turned their attention back to the patient; she had died. More discussion followed about what to do next. I can't remember what happened. I and the others were stunned. But, I had this profound sense that God had not been absent, that in fact, the woman on the cot had been Jesus.

> By "coming to terms with life" I mean: the reality of death has become a definite part of my life; my life has, so to speak, been extended by death, by my looking death in the eye and accepting it, by accepting destruction as a part of life and no longer wasting my energies on fear of death or the refusal to acknowledge its inevitability. It sounds paradoxical: by excluding death from our life, we cannot live a full life, and by admitting death in our life, we enlarge and enrich it.
>
> *An Interrupted Life: The Diaries of Etty Hillesum, 1941-1942*

Joyful Paradox

ooooooooooooooo

To know you is paradox
>To apprehend the cross
>and to know that who is there is you
>To apprehend the cross
>and to know that who is there is me

And everyone else
And all of creation

>To apprehend the cross and to know it
>as unspeakable pain and suffering
>A nightmare from hell

And to know that as you, as me,
as everyone, as all
Far from your protecting us from harm
Quite the contrary

>In order to fill its divine purpose
>Everything must go to crucifixion
>You, me, all of us, the world, the earth
>There is such joy in this knowing.

There is such joy in this knowing
Joy beyond pleasure and beyond delight
in this knowing
To know you as the horror of the cross
is heartbreaking

And yet to know the knowing
of that horrible
heartbreak of you
Is joy
Is from the bottom of my feet joy!
Paradox.

Perhaps it is the utter truth of it all that is so joyful.
Perhaps it is the sublimeness
of your willingness
to suffer yourself
that is so joyful.
Perhaps it is your need and desire
to invite us to suffer
and into the suffering of being your becoming
that is so joyful.
Perhaps it is because your tormented becoming
is so beautiful and so radically alive
that ferments the joy.

I don't know for sure, but I do know
that to gaze upon the cross
And drink it in
Finishes itself in me as joy.
Thou shall love the Lord thy God
with all thy mind and with all thy soul.

Amen, amen, amen.

Dear Elise,

A s you know, in my practice, I see men, women, and lots of couples in lots of dilemmas. Often people will tell me that they are in a relationship extra to their marriage. They are having an affair, and always when that fact is shared, more often than not, they admit to feeling quite torn. They want help in sorting out what to do, which way to go: to the spouse or to the lover. They have a very great deal invested in the marriage and the lifestyle surrounding that marriage, yet there are things wrong with the marital relationship—as there are with all relationships. Some major pieces are missing. On the other hand, the affair brings them something that is new, fresh, alive, growth-producing; it fills in some of the holes in their lives. It wakes up parts of them that have long since been dormant. It arouses creative energies and has some wonderful new possibilities.

What should they do? Should they stay or leave? They can talk about the merits of their spouse and staying with the spouse, and they can talk about the merits of their lover, and ending their marriage and going with their lover. They can go back and forth, and back and forth, and back and forth, between the two possibilities.

> *The solution must rise from the dynamics of the opposing energies that are facing each other.*
>
> *Owning Your Own Shadow*

And then sometimes, they get it. They begin to experience that talking about their spouse and/or their lover, achieves nothing. Yes, they had to do some real-life, practical problem-solving. Yes, they had to make some decisions, but the real issue is not the spouse or the lover; it's their own life. When they get that, when they become aware of that, when that door opens for them, almost miraculous possibilities begin to occur.

I remember saying to one man: "Suppose your wife and your lover were both to die tomorrow. Would that really solve your dilemma?" And he looked at me and said, "No, I'd still be left with my own baggage. I would still have to find out who I really was and what I really wanted and whether either of them or neither of them was who I wanted to be with. Maybe I would want to live by myself. I just don't know. I really don't know who I am." And I said, "Have you really ever wrestled with that question before?" And he said, "No. I guess it's time. What should I do about my marriage and my lover?" And I just looked at him. There was a long silence, and he said, "I knew you would do that. I know the answer already: until I break new ground with myself, I'm not ready or fit to make any decisions about my relationship with either of those two other people. I really have to sit in my own stuff, don't I, no matter how uncomfortable it is, and no matter how long it takes." Then he said, "There really aren't any answers, are there. It's just that the water gets deeper and deeper."

A man named Oedipus came to know all this; he stabs out his eyes. Elise, that is how the story of Oedipus comes to an end. He takes a brooch from the clothing of his mother who has just committed suicide, and with the long clasp pin, he blinds himself.

This is one of the most important stories in the history of mankind, and it is told to us in a trilogy of plays written in Greece many, many centuries ago. They are perhaps the best plays ever written. As the story begins, we are told that Oedipus, a wonderful, brilliant, handsome, young man, has solved the riddle of the Sphinx, making him at least one of the wisest human beings in the world. This is a man truly without faults. He has no tragic flaw. He is a man of moral sensitivity, spiritual integrity, courage, and honesty; he has a beautiful spirit. He is a man who should have been highly favored by God. Oedipus is the natural choice to become a leader, and so he does.

But as events unfold, Oedipus kills the king who also happens to be his father, and marries a woman who also happens to be his mother, has children by her, who are his sons and his brothers. In other words, he commits incest, regicide, and patricide—three of the most horrible things a human being can do. He violates three of the great universal taboos. But all this occurs without any malice or knowledge. Oedipus did not mean to violate those taboos, nor did he have any idea what he was doing. He was totally innocent of intent, malice, or forethought.

> *In a showdown God (Self) favors the shadow over the ego, for the shadow, with all its dangerousness, is closer to the center and more genuine.*
>
> ———
> *Owning Your Own Shadow*

At the end of the play, Oedipus stands beside the body of his suicided mother realizing that, contrary to traditional religious understanding, there is no connection whatsoever between leading a good and righteous life—in his case, a very good and righteous life—and being rewarded or protected by the gods. All his innocence, all his goodness, all his wisdom, all his integrity, all his courage, all his best intentions and soul-searching amounted to nothing. He still committed and was responsible for hideous acts. Life cannot be manipulated by morality or cleverness; life cannot be manipulated by anything.

And thus, Oedipus stands on the stage, in our very midst, and stabs out his eyes. What is the meaning of this hideous act? Modern interpreters have thought it had something to do with guilt or punishment or remorse or regret or penance. Rather, there is another understanding, an understanding based on the awareness that there was a religious group in ancient Greece called "Mystedes" (from which we get the word *mystery*) that intentionally blinded themselves precisely so they would not be distracted by the seeing with visible outer sight, and instead be free, learn to see more profoundly with inner sight, into the mystery of life.

Oedipus knew that life was more profound and more mysterious than the explanations and clichés offered by traditional philosophy or religion. He knew that his soul, the human soul, is vast, complex, and infinite—as vast, complex, and infinite as the nighttime sky. He knew that his life, who he was, and the acts he innocently committed made no sense. So, if he could perhaps penetrate the realities of life more deeply, he might find some locus of meaning. He blinds himself for truth.

If life is not about one-sided morality or intelligence, perhaps inner sight can show what life is really about. Are not each of us, Elise, just like Oedipus, always needing to look through, look beyond traditional understanding and fabricated realities, hoping for a new vision?

Just like Oedipus, most of us experience life as an ongoing series of very difficult dilemmas (which means to be caught on both horns—both sides of an issue at the same time). Even being born, it seems, is experienced by the infant as a dilemma because to be born into life necessitates the departure forever from the wonderful existence of the womb. How often we feel we would sometimes like to return. Sometimes people do partially return. They return in alcohol, in suicide—but then the cost is the loss of conscious life.

Even at the level of the cell, the difficulty of the dilemma is obvious. Watching a cell under a microscope as it is about to split and become two cells, one can see that there is almost the same amount of energy in the cell attempting to keep the cell one, unsplit, united, as there is energy in the cell propelling itself to divide and become two. Dilemma—just when I'm my most creative, I am often reminded of how destructive I can be. Dilemma—just when I am facing how hurtful I am, someone surprises me and tells me how much my love for them has meant. Dilemma—growth.

> *Some of the pure gold of our personality is relegated to the shadow because it can find no place in that great leveling process that is culture.*
>
> Owning Your Own Shadow

So, always and everywhere, you and I and all of us seem to walk and stagger and stumble and leap and bound through this experience of simultaneous, insoluble, internal and external opposites.

And just as it is within you and me, this "conjoining

and conjunction of opposites," so it is between any two people or in larger groups like family or community or the nations of the world. All creation flows in this difficult and troubling, troubling, sometimes lumbering, sometimes exquisite, movement of God's becoming. God is not finished. God is always finishing. Perhaps God has even created evil so that Becoming may proceed, for evil is the most powerful force that can invite and provoke us into becoming more conscious; after all, Lucifer is the "bringer of light." These dilemmas are set up both within us and around us.

In the past, I have tried to deal with this by choosing or identifying with one of the opposites over and against the other. For example, identifying with my creativity and trying to deny, repress, or obliterate my destructiveness. I would try any way to reduce a painful complex duality to a singularity; any strategy to remove me from the tension and pain of dealing with simultaneous opposites.

It's a bit different for me now. I come back to my dream, the dream of the apple and the needle that I had as a young boy. Although it was a recurring nightmare, it was a dream, I believe, that taught me the most important lessons of my life, a dream that prepared me for my career.

The Apple and the Needle

As a small child, I had a recurring dream. It was for me a nightmare, terrifying in its sensations and in its repeated visitations. I dreamed I was standing and looking at my left hand and my right hand both slightly outstretched. In the palm of my left hand was a long, polished, shiny, cold, incredibly sharp, incredibly thin, sewing needle. In the palm of my right hand was a large, round, luscious, red apple. Somehow, I knew that it was absolutely necessary for me to experience simultaneously both sensations of holding the apple and the needle. I was not to let either drop, nor was I to put the needle into the apple. I had to hold onto and feel the roundness and lusciousness and full-bodiedness in one hand and the thinness and coldness and sharpness and metalness in the other. The tension between the two sensations was almost unbearable. I was afraid I could not bear the intensity of the two. I was afraid I would literally be torn apart, ripped down the middle.

Fire Bearer

Now, Elise, when I find myself in one of those horrible difficulties, pulled four ways to Sunday at the same time, I attempt to simply sit in the midst of the tension with as much patience as I am able to muster, to bring into awareness as much as possible each of the options, to deepen my ability to entertain those options with the hope that, by holding the tension and holding all those possibilities, something new, some new possibility, some new vision, some new creative glimmer not before seen, might become apparent. And when and if some third thing emerges that I never before have seen, it is new, and I am new, and then there is something in the world that is also new. I know that process to be the work of God, that I was used by God as a place in which an infinitesimal, small, but nevertheless, real piece of God's own conflicted allness of allness has been brought to resurrectional transformation.

This is the purpose of my life, and I believe that is the purpose of your life, Elise. For example, I feel compelled to write, and at the same time, there is energy within me that feels reluctance and fear and distaste for writing. I write and don't write, write and don't write, wrestle and wrestle. The end result is proving far, far different than what I imagined when I set out; something unpredictable, unforeseen, is evoked from me, out of the tension of opposite and equal energies, to write and not to write.

These energies cannot be from my ego. They are far too deep for that. They must come from within my own creative one. They must represent and reflect the mind of the creator himself/herself. Thus, in bearing them and allowing something to happen because of them and between them, a tiny piece of God has become. Because I sense that in some small way, my struggles with the complexities and paradoxes of life are, in fact, the leading edge of God's own thrusting to become—

> *Do you remember the story of Moses and the burning bush? There are many bushes and much burning; but in this story the bush and the burning overlap; the bush is not consumed and we know that two orders of reality have been superimposed. In a moment we find that God is near—the result of the overlap.*
>
> *Owning Your Own Shadow*

and because there is something about knowing that that moves me to the core and evokes immense love—I am willing to forego the fantasy of solving these dilemmas by becoming one-sided. I am increasingly willing to entertain, consciously and intentionally, all the aspects of a given situation and experience the ensuing anxiety, tension, sometimes even disillusionment. I do this as Holy Writ says, in sure and certain hope of the resurrection.

What comes to mind, Elise, is the drama in the Garden of Gethsemane. After Jesus prays, his dear friend and beloved disciple, Judas, betrays him with a kiss. Is this not the conjunction, and in fact, collision of opposites—deep friendship, a kiss, and betrayal—out of which springs the horror of the crucifixion and then the glory of the resurrection?

Think about God as always becoming, that it is the nature of God to become. God cannot be God unless God becomes; to be all of all means to be never finished. Each completion simply is the starting point for the next process of creation. God's being is becoming, and we understand that the outcome of God's becoming is not known to God beforehand; that for becoming to be true becoming, it has to be something unpredictable. Then we may begin to understand that our lives are about becoming.

So, dear Elise, I invite you to bear the struggles, uncertainties, difficulties, paradoxes, and torments of your life, with, if you can, some grace, curiosity, awareness, and even perhaps joy. For in doing so, you carry a tiny but unique "seedling" of God that you alone can bring to fruition. I suspect that when any of us rejects our role as God-birther, thwarting or aborting this process, something is lost from the universe, something that can never be and will never be replaced. Paradoxically, that terrible loss may simply become the occasion for some other tension of opposites to invite its own becoming.

In the Darkness

०००००००००००००००

THE NOISE WAS STARTLING! It was the phone at two-thirty in the morning. The voice of the young woman was familiar because I had been working with her and her husband as their pastor. I was the associate rector of the local Episcopal parish, and they had come to me for help with their relationship. They were both emotionally volatile and immature, and the marriage was severely troubled. There were major deficiencies in both of them that concerned me.

She was quite upset, one might say even hysterical, begging and pleading with me to come to her home. Her husband was saying terrible things and was threatening to leave. I tried talking her through some of her turmoil on the phone, but to no avail. She insisted that I come right away!

I was young, bright, clever, invulnerable, capable of all things—and afraid to say "no." So, against my better judgment, I said "yes" and found myself dressing, telling my wife where I was going, and heading off in my car to this couple's home.

I rang their doorbell. The husband answered the door in a very contained and composed manner. She was sitting on the sofa, dressed in a flimsy nighty. He asked me to sit down. I did and we talked.

Their argument was going nowhere. In about three minutes, the husband stood up and casually walked over to a piece of many-drawered furniture. While he continued to talk, he opened one of the drawers, pulled out two finely-honed steel-blade hatchets, and came toward me. Before I knew it, one of those hatchets was one-eighth of an inch away from the bridge of my nose, vibrating in the tension of his hand. In a low and collected voice, he said that he'd been practicing with hatchets, that he had sharpened them, and that he and I were going to have a hatchet fight at the end of which one of us would be dead. Clearly, he had gone over the edge; he meant every word of what he said, and I knew that his description of the outcome was a distinct possibility.

His wife continued to sit on the sofa, becoming increasingly hysterical—again—screaming at him that if we were going to have a hatchet fight, we should have it outside because she didn't want blood all over her furniture.

Three options went through my mind:

1. "I'm in pretty good shape. Perhaps we can have a hatchet fight, and I will prevail. I shouldn't let this son of a bitch intimidate me!"
2. "I can use my rudimentary knowledge of psychotherapy to try to help him identify and sort out his anger, rage, and aggression. (The fact that I had any expertise in counseling was one of the reasons he was so angry at me.)
3. "I could blink and pinch myself and I will wake up! It will all go away; it's all a very bad dream."

None of those options seemed very helpful or real, and for a few moments, I was frozen—at a dead end.

Then an option came to mind that I had never in my life thought of before: tell the real truth about myself, a truth that I had never dared acknowledge before. So, I looked up at him, and I said very quietly, "I will not pick up one of the hatchets. If we have a hatchet fight, you'll have to do it by yourself. I know that you are better than I am and that you will win, and that you will kill me, and I am very, very scared."

> *I am Yahweh, and there is no other,*
> *I form the light and I create the darkness,*
> *I make well-being and I create disaster,*
> *I, Yahweh,*
> *do all these things.*
>
> Isaiah 45:6

Quite puzzled and disoriented, he sat down across the room; he had nothing to say. Then, finally, he told me to leave, which I quickly did, getting in my car and going down the street to a friend's house to call the police.

In that moment, a small truth in me died: I was invulnerable. Larger truth had been spoken and given words: I was helpless and terrified and a loser. Both gave me life and, I think, saved my life.

If Rudolf Otto is correct, the experience of the
numinous is at the heart of all true religions.
This we might expect, but Jung went further than
that and said that an experience with numinous was
also at the heart of all valid psychotherapy.
It was Jung's belief that only an experience with the
numinous could truly heal us. Since he believed
God communicated through the unconscious,
he believed this experience could be found through
working with the unconscious and the facts seem
to prove that he was right. The process of
psychotherapy consists of many elements,
but if that therapy includes the unconscious,
then at the heart of it is the experience with the
numinous. It is this that properly orients the ego
toward God, for when we meet the numinous
we know we have met with a greater reality
than our ego and it must be respected, listened to,
and carefully observed for its meaning.
Psychologically, this is the "fear of the Lord"
that is the "beginning of wisdom."

Mystical Christianity

Dear Elise,

ET US LOOK very carefully, very faithfully, and very lovingly, at the real experience of being a human being. What is it, really, to be human? I think we should do this careful examination not just because it is a good thing to know ourselves as well as we can and as honestly as possible, but also because we know that imbedded deeply within our own experience is the presence of God. So that if we look at our own experience as profoundly as possible, we are going to come into the experience and, therefore, the knowing of God.

There have been many attempts to define or describe what it is to be human. For instance, some have pointed to human intelligence, others to our capacity for humor and laughter, and still others to our relentless use of symbol and myth in the service of forging meaning. Others point to our need and ability to act with genuine sacrificial love.

I would like to point to the phenomenon that we, like all of creation, must bear the pain and suffering of the irreconcilable opposites of existence itself. Within us, light and dark, good and evil, love and hate, life and death, are distributed equally. What makes us unique is that we must bear this awful dilemma intentionally, consciously; that is to say, we know this to be true about ourselves, and we know there is ultimately no solution. We also know in our consciousness that our ability to suffer the tension of the irreconcilable opposites in the very nature of our being results in the birthing of new possibilities, new options, new consciousness, which never before existed. Suffering is the necessary precondition to the expansion of consciousness.

So, Elise, as humans, we fully participate and are conscious of the universal cosmic process of becoming; and by virtue of our consciousness, we can just surrender to that process, and actually be lovingly grateful for it.

I would further suggest that this definition of what it is to be human is, in fact, the profound place of depth which reveals to us the true nature of God. Thus, as we develop compassion for ourselves as involuntary bearers of this awful and glorious cosmic birthing process, we can

> *See now that I,*
> *I, am he,*
> *and beside me there is*
> *no other god.*
> *It is I who deal death*
> *and life; when I have*
> *struck, it is I who heal*
> *(no one can rescue*
> *anyone from me).*
>
> *Deuteronomy 32:39*

also begin to grow a deep pathos and empathy for the divine. Our suffering is God's suffering, and God's suffering is our suffering. It costs God to be God, and it is possible to come to know that in your heart and be moved to your core by that—a movement of inner depth that takes you beyond your cares and anxieties for yourself and into a realm of upsurging love and compassion for all creation and, most especially, the creator.

The Dance

○○○○○○○○○○○○○○○

M Y COURAGEOUS AND YOUNGER BROTHER and I were partners in a comic/tragic dance. The choreography is the familiar tango of the so-called dysfunctional family, the first child and the second child, a choreography of tension and opposites which to this day, remains painful, not yet fully resolved between us. Yet, for me—and I hope for him—the tension helped open the door into the great mystery of conscious life itself.

> *God needs humanity in order that he may become fully conscious, and especially to become fully conscious of the absolute opposites that exist in the divine creative potential.*
>
> The Illness That We Are

I was put ahead a grade in school. My brother was put back a grade. My father brought home a new company car, and the next Saturday, I polished the chrome on the front end; my brother, at the back end, poured handfuls of gravel down the gas tank.

One weekday evening, I was at a ceremony at the local elementary school where I was to receive a Cub Scout merit badge. In typical forms of child fashion, I had won so many that I had to wear an extra sash to display them all. My mother was the den mother and was very proud of me. I was very proud of me. I had more virtue badges than any other Cub Scout, and harbored visions of acquiring another sash full.

Just before I was to receive my award, the fire whistle

at the firehouse next door to the elementary school went off; it was the box number of the firehouse itself. There was great commotion, and everybody ran outside to see what was going on. Lo and behold, somebody had gathered a pile of leaves against the backside of the firehouse and had lit it, posing a real threat to the firehouse itself. The fire department quickly had the fire under control, but...it also quickly became very clear that my brother had started the fire. Needless to say, his notoriety that evening far surpassed mine.

We, as a family, lived in the tension of one very deserving, disappointed, self-righteous Cub Scout, and one very clever, angry, famous, soon to have to go to talk to the fire chief, budding pyromaniac. That dance between my brother and me has continued, but we have switched; as my life becomes more and more "outrageous and abnormal," his life becomes more normal and noncontroversial. The universe must require this ongoing and irreconcilable conscious birthing tension of opposites. "Where I am, my brother will always be, and where my brother is, I will always be."

Where Was God?

○○○○○○○○○○○○○○○

THERE ARE MOUNTAINS in Northeast Pennsylvania: the Poconos. Snugly placed near the top of one of these mountains is a retreat center, and on the weekend of June 25-27, 1993, eighty people gathered to celebrate life and explore the theology of the late Anglican theologian William Stringfellow. Some, like Daniel and Phillip Berrigan, had known Stringfellow very well; others, like myself, had simply been inspired and drawn by his written word. Slowly and simply over the weekend, we became a searching and discerning community focusing around the issues of justice, conscience, obedience, peace, social action, the law, all in the context of the gospel.

Due to the conference center's size limitations, I was the only participant sleeping off-campus. Saturday night, following a splendid presentation by a lawyer about William Stringfellow as lawyer and theologian, and the relationship between theology and law (in which the presenter pointed out that the law claims to bring life, but in fact exists to regulate violence through the regulatory tool of violence), I returned to my motel and turned on the television to see a live news conference from the Pentagon. The Chairman of the Joint Chiefs of Staff and the Secretary of Defense were announcing the launch of twenty-three cruise missiles on Baghdad. They justified the attack in the name of international law and order and the eradication of state-sponsored terrorism. The juxtaposition of the people, the words, the witness of the workshop on the mountain, and the news on the TV in the motel room was both jarring and enlivening. My sleep that night was laced with those conflicting realities.

The next morning, returning to the conference center on the mountain to have breakfast with everyone else, I suddenly realized that I alone among those eighty people knew about the events of the prior evening. My sharing the information with one or two people resulted in the conference coordinator requesting that I make a general announcement to everybody. I knew that my words would bring anger and pain and rage to those people, many of whom had risked their lives that this nation not be a purveyor of violence. I knew that they would be particularly vulnerable to this issue.

After I shared the news with great dismay, the group went immediately into a Bible study led by the radiant and faithful mind and spirit of Dan Berrigan. We came to see how Peter and James' public healing of a lame man at the gate of the Temple was not a simple act of restoring someone to health. Nor was it just the transformation of a no-account person into a person of account. It was, in fact, a political act that so threatened and disturbed the powers of law and

> *...as the conscious mind can put the question, "Why is there this frightful conflict between good and evil?", so the unconscious can reply, "Look closer! Each needs the other. The best, just because it is the best, holds the seed of evil, and there is nothing so bad but good can come of it."*
>
> ———
> *Two Essays on Analytical Society*

order, of status quo, that the healers were arrested and brought to trial.

As we were sitting in the main conference room bringing our attention to the biblical passages, the windows were opened for fresh air. On the breath of the fresh air came the sounds of gunfire from the rifle range situated in the valley below the retreat center. On this Sunday morning, this day of rest, this Sabbath, there were those who, for at least two hours, kept at their spiritual discipline of piercing the bull's-eye with the bullet. The firing was incessant. It sounded, I imagine, like combat.

Where was God? Certainly God was with us on the top of the mountain as we devoted ourselves to holy Scripture; certainly God was with our hopes and prayers for peace and justice, for nonviolence and love, for a deeper vision of reality than simply law and order.

> *How ever great one's suffering is, if it comes through God, God suffers from it first.*
>
> Meditations With
> Meister Eckhart

Was God also in Baghdad? Was God on the Navy ships that launched the cruise missiles? Was God in the hands of those who press the buttons? Was God in the White House and at the Pentagon? And was God at the rifle range? Was God in the eye that sights the bull's-eye and the finger that pulls the trigger and the hand that places the bullet in the chamber?

Was God in all those places too? Yes!

Our desire, of course, would be to have it simple, more convenient: God in one place and not the others. Or maybe even God just more in one place and less in others. But the truth is, God is fully in all those places, and I was called, as were the other participants—as are all of us—to bear that irreconcilable conflict: God is in all those places. God is suffering the unbearable, is existing in the excruciating tension of that deep, deep truth. The truth is that in the very tension itself, something utterly new of God, something never before seen of God, will be born, will come forth, and that we ourselves might become the locus of that new truth, that we ourselves might become God-birthers.

Reflections

ooooooooooooooo

To Countess Margot Sizzo-Norris-Crouy
April 12, 1923:

More and more in my life and in my work I am moti-
vated by the endeavor to correct our old repressions everywhere, which have removed and slowly estranged
from us the mysteries by which we might live infinitely
out of the fullness. The terribleness has frightened and
terrified the people: but where is there something sweet
and splendid, which would not ever wear this mask, this
mask of the terrible?...But as soon as we admit to its
terribleness (not as an adversary, for how could we be
equal to it?), but somehow with a confidence that this
very terribleness may be something completely ours, only
for the moment something still too big, too wide, too
incomprehensible for our learning hearts....He who does
not at some time, with definite determination, consent
to the terribleness of life, or even exult in it, never takes
possession of the inexpressible fullness of the power of
our existence, but walks on the edge and will, sometime
when the decision is made, have been neither alive nor
dead.

Selected Letters of Rainer Maria Rilke

The Better I Get,
The Worse I Get

○○○○○○○○○○○○○○○

S HE IS A CLIENT who works hard. She wrestles
not only with her own personal issues but also
with those larger issues implied by life itself.
She is a pleasure to work with. She sees her work in
therapy and her life in a genuinely enlarging religious
context. She's sincere, honest, intelligent, and a bit of a
health nut.

On this day, she comes in with a big smile. She has a
major speech to give to a professional group, and she is
really sweating it. In her reflective and meditative moments, her voice and words are coming to her. She feels
strong, more confident, more articulate, more centered,
and more herself than ever before. She has a voice.

At the same time, she is struggling with her third case
of the flu in as many months. She's even afraid that she
may have pneumonia and has started antibiotics. Being
a health nut, she wonders about stress and diet. Somehow she felt that she ought to be able to keep herself
from getting sick. She has not known herself as a person
who has prolonged illnesses. So this is strange for her,
and it's confusing. She doesn't understand how she can
feel so expanded and enlarged and moving into a new,
powerful, and substantially creative voice while at the
same time, be ill longer than she has ever been ill—with

the threat of a major illness being a distinct possibility. How can both things happen simultaneously?

As she struggles with this paradox, she begins to comprehend and perceive a wisdom that she has only previously brushed up against. "I think I understand. Most of my life has been lived thinking that the goal of my life and anybody's life was to become healthier, more well, more whole, more good, more enlightened, and thus at the same time, to become less evil, less sick, less broken, less unconscious. But my experience is teaching me that you really can't have one without the other; that to go for one in an attempt to obliterate the other, you simply drive the other underground, and out it comes in some worse and horrible way, doesn't it. It's really just two sides of the same coin, and you really can't have one without the other. No wonder I find my voice, my substance, my creativity, and must begin antibiotics at the same time. All of life is like that, isn't it. That's just the way it's put together. All of life is lived somewhere in the middle between the opposites, and there is no escape or solution.

"What is the new direction? It's like that in the world, isn't it. The Berlin Wall comes down. Russian Communism falls apart. The threat of worldwide nuclear annihilation is not so immediate, and we have these most unbearable vicious ethnic civil wars erupting, just like Nazi Germany."

> *Does your heart suffer?*
> *Do the hearts of those*
> *around you suffer?*
> *Then,*
> *you are not yet a mother.*
> *You are still on the way*
> *to giving birth,*
> *You are only near*
> *to birth.*
>
> *Meditations With*
> *MeisterEckhart*

I said to her, "I think you are absolutely right. It reminds me of those times when I have visited people in the hospital who have just discovered that they have a terminal illness and don't have long to live. They are acutely dying; yet, at the same time, very often, they are far more alive than I have ever previously experienced them."

Although it is very right to treat our real disorders and
maximize our health, we make several great mistakes
if we think life should or even can be resolved
to a point of complete serenity and fulfillment.
To believe this is to commit ourselves to a fantasy that
does not exist and that, if it were true, would kill our
love and end in stagnation, boredom, and death.
It is also to remove our concern from the real issues
of our life and world, to transfer our energy to a vague,
self-serving agenda that must be carried out before
we can get on with the business of living, loving,
and creating a better world. Further, the myth
perpetuates the willful delusion that we human beings
are objects, like machines, to be built and repaired,
meant for efficiency rather than love. Most
importantly, the myth of fulfillment makes us miss the
most beautiful aspect of our human souls: our
emptiness, our incompleteness, our radical yearning
for love. We were never meant to be completely
fulfilled; we were meant to taste it, to long for it, and
to grow toward it. In this way we participate in love
becoming life, life becoming love. To miss our
emptiness is, finally, to miss our hope.

The Awakened Heart: Living Beyond Addiction

Strange Birthing

ＯＯＯＯＯＯＯＯＯＯＯＯＯＯ

"**H**AVE YOU EVER SEEN the movie *The Alien?*" he asked. "I feel just like that movie, like there is something growing in me, in my stomach. It's getting bigger. I feel pregnant. I think I'm going to give birth to something. Not necessarily something ugly, like in *The Alien*, but something—and I don't know what it is. I can really feel it. Sometimes it feels like a tight band around the lower part of my chest. There is something in there."

I mentioned to him that in the myths there are all manner of births—both women and men give birth, and they give birth out of all parts of their bodies, not just the vagina.

He went on to say that this growing sense of substance in his gut would "come alive," would "move," would become agitated when he knew that he was hearing or speaking something that wasn't true. He said it was like the wooden nose of Pinocchio. "Furthermore, when I do speak the truth, it seems to be coming from that place; it becomes fully energized." He also noticed how this sensory phenomenon in his body was drawing his attention out of his head and out of concepts down into his body, down into his bowels, and into a different sense of knowing and perceiving and discerning of truth. He said it was like the Chinese understanding of where the true center of the body is, above the genitals and behind the navel: the "dan ting." "Something is getting born in me. I'm going to give birth. I didn't know this was going to happen. I have no control over it. It's going to happen and change my life. I am excited, and I am afraid."

> *The Word of God is always "in the beginning."*
> *And this means*
> *That it is always in the process of being born*
> *And is always already born.*
>
> Meditations With
> Meister Eckhart

My client is in the process of remembering himself, having psychically dismembered himself in childhood, separating his mind from his body; in his remembering is a reconnection to the center of instinctual knowing, and it is a birth—a rebirth, and it will give back to him life and vitality. It will also give God a new pair of eyes, a new set of lungs, a mouth, a heart, a locus to continue the divine becoming.

The cost of this birthing has been high. Years of hard work in therapy, lots and lots of money spent on years of hard work and therapy, which were difficult and painful, the accepting of his life, its paradoxes, dilemmas, complexes, and terrible fears, and finally, the reexperiencing and reevaluating of his relationships with his parents, family, and the women in his life. He vaguely knew that the direction he was going was right for him—while at the same time, often thinking that he or I or perhaps both of us were crazy.

I think now he would say it was worth it.

ooooooooooooooo

When I wake up suddenly in the night with a feeling
of intense despair, with my heart beating fast and
hard, I must remember then that my despair is only
my resistance to suffering. It is my despair at feeling
despair, which prolongs and increases itself.
I must remember then that I am a child of God.
I must surrender myself to whatever suffering
He sends me, take it as a gift, as a friend, even,
sent to me for some reason. The reason why I resist it
so bitterly is because I cling stubbornly to my own
idea of my life, my idea being that I should be
exempt from suffering…that I should be allowed
to work and produce my book.
What good is my book if I don't know enough
to be humble at all times, in all things?
God is with me—controlling me, filling me just as
much when I am suffering as when I am joyous.

The Journals and Letters of the Little Locksmith

Praying for Them

◇◇◇◇◇◇◇◇◇◇◇◇◇◇

THE FOUR DAYS that I prayed for my sisters, children, and friends, I had a hard time with myself. It's hard to stay centered, concentrate on prayers, and keep from being negative.

One great challenge was I prayed alongside a lot of white people who participated in the sacred ceremonies. I prayed for help in knowledge for my people to be free of the past hurts done by these people. I know it's not their fault, but their ancestors', but if they are sorry and want to help, it would be good if they helped by helping set up programs to help with the high alcoholism, violence, unemployment, and housing. Encourage and help with educating our people.

Our people, like my family, are struggling just to get utilities paid, to get food, to buy shoes for Misty or Tim.

And here at the Sundance, I prayed for strength and knowledge and a lot of other things. Here, these people who say they are my friends, come in these expensive R.V.'s, autos, camping equipment, and I listen to them say they sent their children to camp for

> *For suffering smashes to pieces the complacency of our normal fictions about reality, and forces us to become alive in a special sense—to see carefully, to feel deeply, to touch ourselves and our worlds in ways we have heretofore avoided. It has been said, and truly I think, that suffering is the first grace. In a special sense, suffering is almost a time of rejoicing, for it marks the birth of creative insight.*
>
> No Boundary

seven thousand dollars for two weeks. And here's my mother with no food! There were professors, doctors, lawyers, and a couple of movie stars praying with us! Oppression or assimilation in a blend or subtle way?

But, I cried and continued to pray for them and myself. No, I did not envy them or want a brand-new car.

I only wanted peace, love, warmth, and no hunger in homes of my family and the world over, now and in the future.

It is something to work at, hope for, pray for, and live for.

June Lefthand
Lakota Woman

Much of his own writing (Jung) rivets the reader
to the page, rich with the compelling beauty
of his spiritual vision. It is an enticing view
of mankind's potential, borne of Jung's conviction
of the inescapable nearness of the living God.
This God, according to Jung,
authors the conflicts in personal and collective life
in order to complete itself in human life through
more intensely lived and higher unities.
For the Christian to claim entry into the
further reaches of Jung's vision without the painful—
perhaps impossible—facing of the hitherto excluded
Christian shadow would be to betray the ardor
of his spirit for a cheaply gained wisdom and
attenuated sense of the sacred. If we are to truly
assimilate his message, then the reasons for our
current spiritual truncation, the extent of
our one-sidedness, and our prolonged and energetic
fight against the divinely proffered wholeness which
our nature demands must be faced in depth.
This will require what we would all rather avoid:
sustained and soul-searching reflection
of the illness that we are.

The Illness That We Are

The NFL and God

∞∞∞∞∞∞∞∞∞∞∞

Today, I saw you in a thousand faces.
     Foxbow Stadium
The New England Patriots
versus the Houston Oilers
     A sell-out crowd
Men
     Men
Everywhere men
     Eating
Cheering
     Rooting
Drinking
     Especially drinking
Beer after beer after beer
     By the end of the first quarter,
many of the men were unsteady on their feet
     Eyes glazed
Voices louder
     Language cruder and cruder
By halftime,
most of the men were substantially dulled.

     It was unpleasant, unattractive,
       sometimes crude and offensive, stupid.
I have seen too many men that way before.

I had been that way too many times before.
                I was increasingly revolted.
Intelligence and awareness
is won at too high a price.
                But regardless of how revolted
                or offended I was,
                at the same time,
                in every face, in every pair of eyes,
                I saw you.
I saw the pain.
                I saw the longing.
I saw the beauty.
                I saw the vulnerability.
I saw your becoming,
pressing out and through in every face.
                Every face led directly to you.

The contest on the field
was really about you, wasn't it?
                Two teams
Opposing
                Dark and white
Opposite ends of the field
                Both striving to dominate
And nobody knowing the outcome
ahead of time
                And the cheering
The screaming
                The yelling
The booing
                The fanaticism

Really all about you, isn't it?
    Cheering your awful becoming.
I saw a thousand faces today.
    Ugly and offensive
    and filled with your presence.
All that longing leads to you
    All that pain leads to your pain.
Really you were the only one there.

Who Needs Who?

○○○○○○○○○○○○○○○

H E HAS BEEN COMING for a long time, and the focus of his struggle has been vocation. "What is the purpose and meaning of my life? I feel called to something, something sacred, and yet I do not know what it is. I can't find the shape or the form, the handle, an image."

While other issues in this person's therapy had yielded themselves to some loosening and resolution, the issue of vocation has remained very thorny, unresolved, and therefore, poignantly disappointing.

At our previous session, I asked this man if he had the following assumption. I wondered if he was perhaps assuming that the universe, the cosmos, had some preordained goal in mind for him, some preplanned destiny or job description. In other words, did he assume that his vocation was already out there waiting for him to submit? He said, "Yes, indeed." He said that is exactly the assumption he was operating under. He said it was as if the universe had something already planned that he was supposed to do, as if a parent was asking, "What does the universe demand from me?"

> *The need to reestablish the human psyche as the temenos, or container, in which the divine human encounter takes place...*
>
> ―――
> *The Illness That We Are*

I thought for a moment and then made a suggestion: "By reexamining the assumption and changing just a few words in the question, perhaps the stuck place, the locked door around the issue of vocation might open up a little bit." I suggested that he ask this question instead: "What does the universe need from me?"

He looked startled. The idea of the universe needing something from him was strange and foreign; but somehow, as he said it, it was much more on target. "My head says, *How could the universe, all-powerful, all-complete, need anything from me?* But my heart knows that the universe is incomplete, is broken, and is still forming. Of course, it still needs something from me. It needs my caring, but how will I know?"

"With your heart," I said. "If you are able to love the creation and the creator enough, you will know what is needed, and you will be a small but real part of its formation and becoming. You will know in the same manner you know with someone you love. You know what they need before they do."

IV

∘∘∘∘∘∘∘∘∘∘∘∘∘

EMPATHY
AND COMPASSION

∘∘∘∘∘∘∘∘∘∘∘∘∘

Dear Elise,

IN OUR CULTURE, "reality" is marketed on the basis of its utilitarian value. Worth is determined by the answer to the question, "Of what use is this?" Both therapy and religion have fully succumbed to the tyranny of this marketing orientation and have thus sold out. The dominant question in the therapeutic community is "What is the cure and how long will it take?" Usefulness! And in our religious institutions, God is proclaimed "useful" because *God* is the answer for all manner of real or imaginary illnesses and/or difficulties.

The catalog of what therapy or what God can do for us is large and impressive—and it would be wonderful if it were all true. God can help with inner peace. God can help with self-image. God can help with illness. God can help with mortality. God can help with moral dilemmas, and on and on and on. If all the claims for what God or therapy can do for us were true, human life on this planet would be greatly improved and misery would be banished. But how often have we heard the truth-filled question, "How can a good God, a loving, all-powerful, and useful God, let this happen?"

> *And if God does not help me to go on, then I shall have to help God.*
>
> An Interrupted Life:
> The Diaries of Etty Hillesum,
> 1941-1943

Perhaps, if we were to tell the truth, we might dare to acknowledge that God is not very useful. God is, in fact, useless. God is not for our use! Life is not a problem, and God is not the answer. To conceive and proclaim life as the problem and God as the useful answer is to be forced into concocting an ever-deepening sewer of lies, distortions, rigid ideologies, and profound disappointments.

A young Jewess writing from a German prison camp knew how useless God is, and loved God with her whole heart.

I shall try to help You, God, to stop my strength ebbing away, that I cannot vouch for it in advance. But one thing is becoming increasingly clear to me: that You cannot help us, that we must help You to help ourselves. And that is all we can manage these days, and it is also all that really matters: that we safeguard that little piece of You, God, in ourselves. And perhaps in others as well. Alas, there doesn't seem to be much You yourself can do about our circumstances, about our lives. Neither do I hold You responsible. You cannot help us but we must help You and defend Your dwelling place inside us to the last.

An Interrupted Life:
The Diaries of Etty Hillesum,
1941-1943

> There is, in truth, a secret message, explanatory of the whole Creation, which by allowing us to feel God in everything we do and in everything that is done to us (God creating in all things and being born in all things) can bring true happiness to our generation.
>
> *Meditations With Teilhard de Chardin*

God is not for our use, and thus there is no point in trying to make deals with God for this life or the next. Since God is useless and helpless, how can it be said, "If I come to know God, I will love God with all my heart and all my soul and all my mind"? Part of the answer lies precisely in the fact that God is useless. You cannot love, it is not possible to love, that which you are trying to beg from or manipulate.

○○○○○○○○○○○○○○

Faith would be that God is self-limited utterly
by his creation—a contraction of the scope of his will;
that he bound himself to time and its hazards and
haps as a man would lash himself to a tree for love.
That God's works are as good as we make them.
That God is helpless, our baby to bear,
self-abandoned on the doorstep of time,
wondered at by cattle and oxen. Faith would be
that God moved and moves once and for all
and "down" so to speak, like a diver,
like a man who eternally gathers himself for a dive
and eternally is diving, and eternally splitting
the spread of water, and eternally drowned.

Holy the Firm

Redemptive Suffering

○○○○○○○○○○○○○○○

TODAY I SAW A MAN who I've been seeing for a number of years. It has finally come into his consciousness, with a sharp degree of clarity, how he has been taking on and internalizing the fundamental two-sided dilemma of his parents' marital relationship. He saw how he has impaled himself, crucified himself as it were, on the axis of the dynamic forces of their relationship.

His mother is an intelligent, dominating, overbearing, judgmental, perfectionist; his father is immature, sometimes playful, but rebellious, and resistant to his wife's insistence and pressure. His father was so rebellious and resistant that he was willing to both actively and passively allow his physical well-being to degenerate under his own nose and before the very eyes of his wife and son. So the son is both ruthlessly judgmental toward himself and everybody else. He formulates strategies for living which he knows ahead of time will not succeed, and in fact, will lead to some form of deterioration. He is alienated from his mother, and his father has

> *Both (Eckhart and Jung) would agree that God was compelled to create humanity in order to become fully conscious in it. To this basic agreement Jung would add that a major feature in the divine compulsion is God's necessity to constellate and resolve in human consciousness the contradiction divinity itself could neither perceive nor resolve in its own life.*
>
> *A Strategy for a Loss of Faith: Jung's Proposal*

long since died of the physical deterioration. The power and intensity of their relationship—their mutual death dance—has been carried in his psyche and body, lo these many years.

Like most children, this man picked up this parental dilemma as a young child, not simply because he was raised in its environment, but more profoundly, because by choosing to carry it, to bear it, to suffer it, to live it, the child imagines that he (or she) can redeem it, fix it, heal it.

As long as this man remained unconscious of the dilemma that he had taken onto himself, however, he would forever present the stalemating and fragmenting dynamics of his parents' relationship, both in his own interpersonal relationships and his intrapsychic dynamics. He would repeat the dilemma over and over and over again—as if by bearing the suffering of the dilemma unconsciously forever, it would somehow lighten and relieve his parents of their pain.

> *I shall have to learn this lesson, too, and it will be the most difficult of all, "Oh God, to bear the suffering that you have imposed on me and not just the suffering I have chosen for myself."*
>
> An Interrupted Life:
> The Diaries of Etty Hillesum,
> 1941-1943

In therapy, the man gradually became aware of this whole ball of wax and began to move that which had been unconscious into his consciousness. He was able to talk about it, name it, describe it, understand it, and feel it. The nature of the suffering then changed; he no longer has to forever repeat the pattern in his own life. His suffering now consists of feeling his mother's pain and frustration, his father's pain and rage, and his own pain and anger and terror as a little boy caught up in that environment. His pain is the grief of knowing and accepting that things will never ever be any better for his parents, accepting that he could not years ago, and cannot now, help them.

The final stage for this person will be the developing of compassion for himself. He had to endure all that throughout his growing-up years—*and* he is not a failure because he was unable to "fix things" for his parents. This second manner of suffering is redemptive. He makes conscious what the parents had kept unconscious. He bears the suffering which accompanies that courageous act, and some new freedom to live life is inhaled. The way he internally holds and understands reality is subtly, but profoundly and permanently, reshaped, and there is thus even some small difference in the universe.

The Mirror

ooooooooooooooo

Dear Jesus:

What did you say "yes" to
   in the Garden of Gethsemane
      that magnificent night
      so many years ago?

You knew something, didn't you?

              You knew something about God.

You knew that God needed something
   that only you could give,
   and you could only give it
           by saying "yes" to the crucifixion.

You know, dear Jesus, that we say,
   if you want to know who God is,
   simply gaze upon the cross,
      the cross of that Friday on Golgotha,
         that image, that reality
         we claim and proclaim
         as the image and reality of God.
But Jesus, I wonder if that was for us to see.
   Did you do that for the eyes of humans alone,

the most important observers?
Was it our witness that really mattered?

It was God who needed to witness.
I suspect that you knew that God
needed to see that reflection of Self.
That God needed to see
a dimension in and through you,
a dimension that God
had never seen before.

I suspect that God was requiring,
in becoming,
a making conscious of who God really is,
of what it is to be
God-who-becomes.

I suspect that God had known Self
as was described
by those who came before you, Jesus:
good, powerful, loving,
victorious, angry, great sky-parent;
and you knew God's need
to see Self more completely,
more deeply, more fully;
and so you showed God pain.

You showed God excruciating pain,
protracted suffering, helplessness,
vulnerability, despair, betrayal,
frailty, woundedness, hopelessness,

and death,
—and God looked and saw Godself,
and knew for the first time, consciously
the cost of being a God
who ever becomes,
who knew for the first time
the fullness of the opposites
that was God.

You were God's mirror, and through that mirror,
God knew the incredible
rending and tension and anguish
of containing all those opposites.

And that is our job, is it not,
to reflect the opaqueness of our own creation
to the creator,
and thus be the creator's
becoming?

You loved God that much—that much—
to climb up on the cross
for all to see,
but most especially
to show to God
who God really is.

Community or Communion?

oooooooooooooooo

In his Calcutta address, Thomas Merton made
the point that "the deepest level of communication is not communication, but communion.
It is wordless. It is beyond words. It is beyond
speech and it is beyond concept. Not that we
discover a new unity. We discover an older unity.
My dear brothers, we are already one. But we
imagine that we are not. And what we have to
recover is our original unity. What we have to
be is what we are."

Follow the Ecstasy

T HER THIRD SESSION WITH ME, she talked
about how lonely and isolated she felt, how
cut off from her family. In particular, she
suffered a silent distance from her mother which she
couldn't understand. She only knew it hurt a lot. "It's
been so long since I heard someone say to me, 'I love
you.'"

At her fourth session, she came through the door
beaming; her mother had called. The months of silence
had been broken, and she shared: "Just before my mother
hung up, she said, 'I love you.'"

Then with a quizzical look, she asked, "You didn't
call my mother, did you?"

She knew I hadn't, but it was as if some unconscious
connection had been made.

Early on in our work together, he began to tell me about his father. He thought maybe his father lived somewhere in Montana or Utah. He hadn't heard from him or spoken to him in years, and mostly that had been just fine. But now, he felt like it was time for things to be somehow different. He was curious. He would like to make contact with his father if it were possible, but he knew that was a hopeless dream; he had no idea where to start. He wasn't sure he even knew his father's name.

> *We are all of us together carried in the one world-womb; yet each of us is our own little microcosm in which the Incarnation is wrought independently with degrees of intensity and shades that are incommunicable.*
>
> *Meditations With Teilhard de Chardin*

The next session he came in saying, "You'll never guess who called me! My father! He said he started thinking about me—just out of the blue—feeling that it was time to reconnect."

My client looked at me and asked if I had in some mysterious way made contact with his father because he knew some connection had been made.

ooooooooooooooo

The Church talks about community. It refers to itself as the "community of faith" or the "Church family." Towns have community centers, and much time in psychotherapy is spent in looking at and trying to heal and build interpersonal relationships in communities, particularly the small communities of our lives. The need for community or something like it is huge. The failure of human communities to fill that need is, likewise, huge. People belong to this and that organization, club, family, relationship, church, and they are more often than not, dissatisfied, even hurt and wounded. Whatever we are looking for seems, at best, to be only partially filled or perhaps only hinted at in human community.

It seems as if whenever we intentionally try to make community happen, we end up forcing something that turns out to be in the long run, disappointing and destructive. All community, large or small, eventually falls prey to the dynamics of institutional maintenance and deterioration of reverence for the soul. It is not surprising, therefore, that Jung said all individuation is away from the community. Nor is it surprising that Christ said, "The Sabbath is made for man, not man for the Sabbath." In spite of the Church's obsessive value of family, we need to remember that Christ rejected family when he looked at his mother and brothers and said, "This is not my mother, these are not my brothers, this is not my family." Biological linkage as a definition of community was displaced by Jesus in favor of something more important and more powerful.

What might that be?

Perhaps we can sharpen our focus by moving our attention away from human-created community to focus on God-gifted communion. We think we are trying to create something

From the human perspective it means that consciousness can no longer evade its basic task in history, that of serving as the vehicle of God's becoming fully conscious.

A Strategy for a Loss of Faith: Jung's Proposal

new, when in reality, we are looking to rediscover and live into something very old.

The Buddhists talk about a network of lifelong spiritual friendships. We all have people in our lives with whom we feel communion—a communion that is created and fueled by the grace of God. It is nothing that we have made happen. Why not seek out and tend those relationships?

Then there is, of course, the communion among all human beings as brothers and sisters, the communion of human beings with all other living species, and the communion of the living and the dead, the communion of saints. We do not have to create community as if communion did not already exist. We need to acknowledge, instead, the communion that is already present, to know that no matter how profound the suffering or egregious the evil, that we are—all of us—somehow woven into a profound mystical fabric.

vi

Agnus Dei

ooooooooooooooooo

Given that lambs
are infant sheep, that sheep
are afraid and foolish, and lack
the means of self-protection, having
neither rage nor claws,
venom nor cunning,
what then
is this "Lamb of God"?

This pretty creature, vigorous
to nuzzle at milky dugs,
woolbearer, bleater,
leaper in air for delight of being,
   who finds in astonishment
four legs to land on, the grass
all it knows of the world?
       With whom we would like to play,
whom we'd lead with ribbons, but may not bring
into our houses because
it would soil the floor with its droppings?

What terror lies concealed
in strangest words, *O lamb*
of God that taketh away
the Sins of the World: an innocence

smelling of ignorance,
born in bloody snowdrifts,
licked by forebearing
dogs more intelligent than its entire flock put together?

God then,
encompassing all things, is
defenseless? Omnipotence
has been tossed away, reduced
to a wisp of damp wool?

And we,
frightened, bored, wanting
only to sleep till catastrophe
has raged, clashed, seethed and gone by without us,
wanting then
to awaken in quietude without remembrance of agony,

we who in shamefaced private hope
had looked to be plucked from fire and given
a bliss we deserved for having imagined it,

is it implied that *we*
must protect this perversely weak
animal, whose muzzle's nudgings
suppose there is milk to be found in us?
Must hold to our icy hearts
a shivering God?

So be it.

Come, rag of pungent
quiverings,
         dim star.
                  Let's try
      if something human still
      can shield you,
                    spark
      of remote light.

Candles in Babylon,
"Mass for the Day of St. Thomas Dydimus"

CANTICLE V

To Eat Suffering

ooooooooooooooo

It is with new ears and new eyes
That I approach your table
So simply set
With mere bread and wine
> In prior times, the bread and the wine
> were imagined by me to be food—
> your body and blood
> that would feed me,
> strengthen me, protect me, cleanse me,
> nurture me, change me.
I was free to come if I wanted, or if I felt the need.

> And then I began
> To understand
> That the body was broken
> And the blood is spilt
Some terrible disaster had taken place here.
I thought perhaps I was being fed
with the suffering and brokenness
of fellow human beings.
> Of brothers and sisters
> Perhaps even my own brokenness.
But now with these new eyes and new ears
Which you have given me
I see the bread

And I see the wine, I hear the words
>I hear the story
>All anew
>And I know now that it is your woundedness
>Your broken body
>Your spilt blood
>That you are offering me.
You're asking me to eat of you,
to ingest your hurt and pain,
your suffering,
the suffering of the Word becoming Flesh.
To participate with you—not for me, but for you.
>You ask me, you offer me, you command me
>To ingest your pain
>To carry your woundedness
>To suffer your suffering with you
>And somehow
>To render it more bearable for you
The ultimate mystery without answers
We are called to bear your mystery

>And Thus You Become.
And could my life—any life
Have any more
Glorious
Purpose?
>I think not.
Thank you!
I will come to your table again and again.

God's Cutting Edge

ooooooooooooooo

THE WORDS TO THE SONG he was singing were "By the rivers of Babylon, how can we sing a song when we are in exile?"

To be sure, it was his own rendition of a biblical passage, but he was trying to tell me a deep truth about his life. He is a man ordained in the ministry of one of the liturgical denominations, who for reasons of faith, can no longer tolerate exercising his ministry within the boundaries of the visible, institutional Church. He describes himself as having been sitting in a dinghy tethered to a large dock, not a dock that he liked very much, but at least it gave him a point of reference, a sense of orientation, a framework, a container. Then, suddenly, someone cut the rope and the dinghy was drifting free and loose; while he was in the same dinghy, he felt disoriented, lost, without a container. I offered the metaphor of being a photograph, a very nice photograph, but one without a frame or photo album. He is out of context, disoriented. He sees himself sitting by the rivers of Babylon in exile, without a song.

As he was talking, I remembered the group of ten people I had been on retreat with the previous weekend. Most of them hadn't known one another prior to the weekend. They were held together by a common sense that they had been called to ministry in some kind of professional, ordained, public, official way, and yet, in good faith, and because of their faith, they could imagine no way of preparing for or expressing that ministry in and through the forms of the traditional institution.

Like the man with whom I was talking, they had spiritual fire in them that was burning bright—and they had spiritual anguish in them that was loud and painful. They knew themselves called, yet they knew of no way to express that call. They wanted the discernment, training, validation, and celebration of their calling that an institution can give them, but they didn't want to have to compromise themselves to an institution that will somehow diminish them, demean them, and depress them.

They were looking for God. They were looking for answers, and yet, as I looked at them, I realized that they were the answer, and in fact, they were God. They were God becoming. They didn't have the answers; I didn't have the answers. The Church didn't have the answers. Yet each of them, in his or her own way, will have to be—cannot help but be—faithful to that sense of call. How each, with courage and perhaps help and discernment from other people, works out the struggle and answers the questions will become the answer for a new form of ministry never before seen. For, in fact, there is no prior or old form of official ministry into which they can easily slip. They have to become the new form themselves. It was

> *I am more and more convinced that the great event of our time is a kind of change in the face of God in which the pure "God of above" of yesterday is being combined with a kind of "God of ahead" (In the extension of the Human).*
>
> Meditations With
> Teilhard de Chardin

as if I were watching God trying to emerge, trying to become some new shape, some new manifestation. As each struggled with all this, we as a community realized that we were taking on some new shape. We were being newly formed in ways that we did not fully understand. They/we/us were pregnant with God, and the anguish of those people that weekend and the anguish of the man I was talking with is nothing less than the labor pains of the One who says, "I am whatever I become; I make all things new!"

September 1, 1939

∘∘∘∘∘∘∘∘∘∘∘∘∘∘∘

From the conservative dark
Into the ethical life
The dense commuters come,
Repeating their morning vow,
"I *will* be true to the wife,
I'll concentrate more on my work,"
And helpless governors wake
To resume their compulsory game:
Who can release them now,
Who can reach the deaf,
Who can speak for the dumb?

All I have is a voice
To undo the folded lie,
The romantic lie in the brain
Of the sensual man-in-the-street
And the lie of Authority
Whose buildings grope the sky:
There is no such thing as the State
And no one exists alone;
Hunger allows no choice
To the citizen or the police;
We must love one another or die.
Defenceless under the night
Our world in stupor lies;

Yet, dotted everywhere,
Ironic points of light
Flash out wherever the Just
Exchange their messages:
May I, composed like them
Of Eros and of dust,
Beleaguered by the same
   Negation and despair,
   Show an affirming flame.

Selected Poems of W.H. Auden

Terrifying Knowing

○○○○○○○○○○○○○○

I hear you...I hear you.
> I hear you in my chest,
> in my heart,
> and behind and in my eyes.

I hear you in my jaw, in my throat,
and in my shoulders,
and in my groin.
> I hear you in my belly.

Mostly, I hear you in my chest.

> Because I hear you, I know you.

I know you, and it is true
that you knew me
in my mother's womb.
> I know you, and it is true
> that you are closer to me
> than I am to myself.

And because I hear you and know you,
I am more and more
in spite of myself
coming to love you
> with all my heart,
> and with all my soul
> and with all my mind.

All my life, I have felt
a huge well-spring of love for you
at the center of my being.
      That fact is the most terrifying fact of my life.

I know you, and now
I am able to allow
that well-spring.
      Because I hear you and I know you,
      I also know what you are
      and what you are *not* saying.

In my hearing of you,
I know that you need and want something
from me,
from all of us.
      And in my knowing of you,
      I am so moved by you
      that I cannot help but give you
      what you need.
I hold the hearing and knowing of you as precious.
      I hold your needing of me as precious.

ooooooooooooooo

Rather here Jung's understanding entails
a radically new paradigm which would insist that
God and human consciousness are so intimately—
I would suggest ontologically—linked that they are
best understood as "functions" of each other.
This intimacy supposes a mutual dependence and
interaction which might accurately be described by
both Eckhart and Jung as a process of mutual
redemption....Rather, this newer paradigm
necessarily implies the creation of human
consciousness as the needed cooperant
on whom divinity is dependent for divinity's
redemption in the human.

A Strategy for a Loss of Faith: Jung's Proposal

The Eucharist

○○○○○○○○○○○○○○

WE SAT TOGETHER almost forty years later, circling a low table, Ota, Mr. Masako, a reporter who, like me, wanted to make a record of this story, Becky, who interpreted for me, and Mr. Kikawa, director of this school, once an orphanage for children cast into a state of abandonment by the explosion of the atomic bomb over Hiroshima. The island of Ninoshima had to be cleared of corpses to make way for the children, several weeks after the bombing. Years later, mass burial sites were still being discovered. "Now to speak of it," he told us, "is almost unbelievable."

They lay there, Ota and the others who were wounded and dying, endlessly, day after day. A list of names was posted. Each time someone died, another name was struck from the list. Many vomited blood or lost hair. Bodies were swollen. These are symptoms of radiation poisoning. Burns became infected and filled with pus. Maggots grew in the open, unhealing wounds. Ota told me he believes he survived only because his younger brother picked the maggots from his body every day. Those with no one to do this died. Because of his burns, he lay on his left side. In this way, as it healed, his ear was fixed to the back of his head, as it still is today. His mouth was filled with dust unsettled by the blast. But he had been told not to drink the water.

All over Hiroshima people were warned about the water. Those too badly injured to move would cry out again and again for water that never came. And in moments of extreme pain, people of all ages would cry for their mothers.

How did he beat the pain? Everyone was in the same pain, he said. At times they would cry out together. The most severely injured could not cry. Over time, it was better for all of them to lie there quietly. Then, the pain was felt, not as if in one body alone, but in all bodies at once. Together they floated in a timeless element, suffused with agony, ringed with death, held in one another's presence.

Chorus of Stones: The Private Life of War

ooooooooooooooo

The powers
that we have released,
could not possibly be absorbed
by the narrow system of individual
or national units
which the architects of the human Earth
have hitherto used.
The age of nations has passed.
Now, unless we wish to perish,
we must shake off our old prejudices
and build the Earth.

Meditations With Teilhard de Chardin

A Lover's Cup

◌◌◌◌◌◌◌◌◌◌◌◌◌◌

Dear Jesus,

I must think about you two or three times every day; somehow you keep coming into my mind. I often find myself wondering what it was really like for you? What did you really say? What was life like two thousand years ago? How was it to be inside your consciousness?

Mostly I'm intrigued about the night you were arrested, that moment in the Garden when you prayed by yourself, when you said, "Take this cup from me."

What kind of cup was it?

Was it a sinister cup laced with the toxins of one who sought to assassinate you?

Was it the cup of bitter herbs which Socrates was forced to drink?

Was it the cup of a priest who offers to his spiritual children sacramental drink for the soul?

Or was it a lover's cup—a cup of invitation, enticement, and intoxication?

And when you paused and sweat and then said, "Not my will be done, but thine," what power, what force, what necessity were you speaking from? Did you feel compelled out of some rigid orthodoxy, cosmic destiny, pietistic obligation? Were you coerced into obedience and surrender? Or was this an act of will, of choice of freedom—perhaps it was a cry of ardor, of wooing, a lover's response? And in spite of the fact that it was going to cost you everything, the love of the one you loved was even more compelling.

A lover's cup, and a lover's cry—"Yes, yes, yes, and again I say, yes!"

You must have known God. Not known about God, but known God in the most immediate and intimate of ways. I suspect that your knowing of God began early in your life, very early, and that your knowing was loving, and that your knowing and loving of God came almost to completion on the Mount of Transfiguration because from that point onward in your life, your loving of God compelled you toward Jerusalem. The one you loved so much somehow required you there at Golgotha on the cross, and you could not say "no."

What did the one you loved need from you? How was the One for whom you had so much passion more fully loved by your willful actions of bringing about your own crucifixion? How did your action love the Holy One more? What need in the Holy One was filled by your desperate and utter act of self-abandonment? You gave completely to the One you loved, and you gave something evidently only you could give, and you gave something that required a complete giving, and you gave something that the Holy One required, something that if we loved the Holy One with all our heart and all our mind and all our soul, we would desperately want to give regardless of the cost.

Yes, you must have known God ever so deeply. Was God changed by your love and your act? I believe so.

Is there something about the Holy One still to this day which evokes that self-same self-emptying love from those of us who know and love? Yes, I believe so.

What is it about the Holy One that you knew? What is it about the Holy One that makes us want to give everything though it would break our hearts, maybe end our lives? What is it about the Holy One, Jesus, son of Joseph, that moves us so deeply that we cannot wait but to bear tremendous suffering? If only it would be to the Holy One as love.

Who Loves Who?

oooooooooooooo

T HIS PARTICULAR weekly therapy group has been meeting for quite some time; the bonding and trust among the members is real and deep.

There is a woman in the group who is lovely, very intelligent, insightful, courageous, committed to the therapeutic process, and deeply respectful and caring of the other members of the group.

At the same time, she is not able to love herself; no matter how specifically members of the group tell her that they experience her as lovable. In fact, when members of the group tell her they love her, she cannot find a way to take that inside and feel it apply to herself. She has no knowing of herself as loved, regardless of the energy and effort by those in the group to convince her otherwise.

Yet, she is very able to experience and talk about her love for some of the people in the group. It is more than obvious. She listens exquisitely well, treats people with great respect, and says that she genuinely loves them; she can feel that love in her body and knows it is real. She is able to love others, even though she cannot experience, feel, or receive their love for her.

One evening in group, this woman began to talk about a new boyfriend, describing him in the most glowing of terms. He sounded very attractive. Someone asked her if she loved him, and if she did, why. She became embarrassed and said that she did love him, adding "Because he loves me." She couldn't really feel his love, but she thought it was nice to be loved. She was embarrassed because she knew that loving someone simply because that person loves you first is not a solid or mature way of building a relationship. She wondered whether there was anything about her boyfriend that was essential to him that would cause her to love him regardless of how he felt about her. She could not receive or experience love. She was very capable of loving, and she knew that loving people simply because they said they loved her first was shallow.

Our human experience is like hers; when someone deeply and steadfastly loves us, it doesn't automatically mean we will feel ourselves loved. Yet, even when we experience ourselves as unlovable and unloved, we are capable of real and intense love for others.

> *Jung sums this up in his own terms: "Here Eckhart states bluntly that God is dependent on the soul, and at the same time, that the soul is the birthplace of God."*
>
> *A Strategy for a Loss of Faith: Jung's Proposal*

Love is the central concept of the New Testament; how often have we said, "God so loved the world that he gave his only begotten Son, and therefore, we are to love God?" How often have we said, "We should love God because God loved us first?"

I don't know if God loves me. I'm not sure about that, and as near as I can tell, I don't particularly care. What I do know is that I love God, and I love God whether or not God loves me—and not because God loved me first, but because God is so profoundly lovable, so profoundly compelling. I don't expect God to do anything for me.

Loving God is not about begging, manipulating, bargaining. If I thought I could beg, manipulate, or bargain with God so that God would somehow do something for me or make a situation better for me, I think I would be afraid of God. I would resent God. I would think less of God. I'm pretty sure I would not love God.

So the question is, "What about God makes God so profoundly and movingly lovable?" I suppose we must each answer that question ourselves, individually, and each of us must answer it out of our own experience.

For me, to know God is to love God, and to know God and love God is to impact God; God wants that and asks that from me. God is vulnerable to my love. To know God is to love God is to change God is to want to give God whatever God needs from me.

ooooooooooooooo

I embark on a slow voyage of exploration with
everyone who comes to me. And I thank YOU
for the great gift of being able to read people.
Sometimes they seem to me like houses with open
doors. I walk in and roam through passages
and rooms, and every house is furnished a little
differently and yet they are all of them the same,
and everyone must be turned into a dwelling
dedicated to YOU, oh God. And I promise You,
yes, I promise that I shall try to find a dwelling
and a refuge for You in as many houses as possible.
There are so many empty houses, and I shall prepare
them all for You, the most honored lodger.

An Interrupted Life:
The Diaries of Etty Hillesum, 1941-1943

The Certainty of You

ooooooooooooooooooo

When I look at the world, I see you.
I see you by the wounding, the sorrow,
the depravity,
. the evil, the tragedy.
> The worse it becomes,
> the more I'm sure of you.
> It is all the necessity and urgency
> of your becoming.
What a terrible, terrible price
you are willing to pay
to be faithful to your own nature
of becoming.
> Because it's all about you,
> it is all simultaneously filled with beauty,
> the miracle of love, tender mercies, and grace.

What a wonderful thing you have done
to invite us and even make it a requirement
that we may and must participate with you
in your becoming.
> To weep and bleed with you
> To watch and bear witness with you
To laugh and dance with you
To suffer and carry it for you
> To anticipate with you

the unknown becoming
Which measured by
the immensity of the suffering
must be beyond measure.

Your willingness to be faithful to yourself
regardless of the cost
moves in me so deep.
So very deep.
> That while I know I have a choice
> I feel no choice.
> But to say, "yes."
> To continue in the eating of the wafer
> and the drinking of the wine.

Dear Elise,

S O ELISE, by now one or two things about me must be obvious. It must be obvious that I believe in God, or rather that I put my belief into God. Or even better yet, that I experience God. I know with all my being—and all my being knows—there is an ongoing process, power, presence, that moves me, compels me, intrigues me, enlivens me, humbles me, and evokes more from me than I ever thought was there. This I call God, and I would have to deny my own existence if I were to deny God. This presence engages me in such a way that I respond with feelings, images, behaviors, thoughts, and words. So while I know it is not a person, still somehow, there is a consciousness that has a personal dimension which evokes my personhood.

It also must be obvious to you that I find human life (and probably all life among other things) to be a terrible struggle; a struggle caused by and lived out in a seemingly infinite set of ongoing irreconcilable opposites, a terrible struggle filled with tension. Many people see this struggle and tension as the quintessential problem of life, and expect God and/or therapy to cure, fix, or change it. But what if, instead

> *Up until now, to adore has meant to prefer God to things by referring them to God and by sacrificing them to God.*
> *Now adoration means the giving of our body and soul to creative activity, joining that activity to God to bring the world to fulfillment by effort and intellectual exploration.*
>
> *Meditations With Teilhard de Chardin*

of asking "What can we do to fix it or change it?" "How did it get this way?" and "What did I do to deserve this?" we ask another question entirely? What happens if we accept life as it is, as a given, and ask the question, "Why is existence and human life the way it is?" Let us suppose that it is as it should be, and it is serving some purpose. What happens if, instead of seeing life as a problem that needs to be fixed or solved, we see it as the answer? What happens when we take human beings out of the center and put God in the center? What happens if we become genuinely theocentric: God-centered? What happens if, instead of seeing God as existing primarily to take care of our needs, we begin to understand that perhaps creation is a response to God's needs—creation and human existence as it was, is, and is becoming—a just right response to God's needs.

So, what can we say about God in all this?

I've come to understand that the struggle and the tension is, in fact, the birthplace of life itself, and human life in particular—and more particularly, the birthplace of ever-growing divine/human consciousness. Not only is God not the cure or the fix for this paradox and mystery we call life but, in fact, God is the creator of it, the one who necessitates it, and the one who benefits most from it. Your life, my life, Elise, all our lives, are exactly as God needs them to be—tension-filled struggles of tumultuous opposites.

> *I so wish I could put it all into words. Those two months behind barbed wire have been the two richest and most intense months of my life, in which my highest values were so deeply confirmed. I have learned to love Westerbork.*
>
> *An Interrupted Life: The Diaries of Etty Hillesum, 1941-1943*

The infinitude of God has something to do with encompassing a "space" large enough to hold all these opposites, and the opposites of the opposites. The Hindus know something of this in that they have an uncountable number of gods, each one reflecting a face or an aspect of God. The Chinese often speak of their gods, each being capable of coming to us in either a light and light form or a dark and heavy form, depending. In the Old Testament, God sometimes refers to Self as "we," and in the New Testament Jesus says about God, "In my Father's house are many mansions."

> *When I suffer for the vulnerable, is it not for my own vulnerability that I really suffer?*
>
> *An Interrupted Life: The Diaries of Etty Hillesum, 1941-1943*

To be God, it seems, is to be all, not some of all, not the simple dimensions of all that we are most comfortable with, but all of all. I believe, therefore, that anything we say about God, we also must be prepared to say and hear the opposite. So, when we speak of God as all, we also speak of God as not. When we speak of God as light, we must also speak of God as dark. And yes, of course, then we find ourselves led into ways of talking about God that are difficult and hard and uncomfortable. Perhaps we even end up speaking in silly semantic word games.

By virtue of the fact that God is totally caught up in becoming, we, too, are becoming—becoming in a way that leaves us absolutely and literally without a clue as to what the next turn of events holds for us.

In one way, Elise, that makes our lives quite wonderful and exciting and remarkable. It means that we are not caught forever in some self-repeating pattern of stuckness; to change and be changed is possible. It means that we never know the final chapter; that it's really not over until it is over. I think it means that the experience of living, despite our best efforts, is very, very frightening, very, very terrifying; our lives are absolutely unpredictable. No matter how well we understand ourselves, how deeply we delve into our past, how much we heal the wounds of our history and forgive ourselves and others for being victims and/or perpetrators, there is simply no way to know, predict, or control what the next moment will bring. Our futures are full of wonderful and terrifying—and infinite—possibilities.

God is not useful. God is not helpful. God is not for our use or for our help. We are for God's use and God's help. In the language of therapy, reality is not for our use; it is not useful or helpful. We are for reality's use and help. What a liberation it is to be lifted out of the dead-end paradigm of the ego's anxieties over its own existence by virtue of the discovery that we are for God's/reality's use.

What of love? What of empathy? What of compassion? I'm told to love God because God first loved me. But that simply is not true to my experience. I don't love people because they first loved me. I love them because I love them. I don't suspect Jesus surrendered his life to God because God first loved him. Jesus surrendered his life to God simply because he overwhelmingly and outrageously loved God.

> *I shall merely try to help God as best I can and if I succeed in doing that, then I shall be of use to others as well.*
>
> ---
>
> *An Interrupted Life: The Diaries of Etty Hillesum, 1941-1943*

I don't love God because God is useful or helpful or lovable. I don't love God because God is not useful or helpful or lovable. I just find God utterly and compellingly provoking my love, my empathy, my compassion.

Thou shalt love the Lord thy God with all thy heart, with all thy mind, and with all thy soul.

CANTICLE VIII

Body Knowing

ooooooooooooooo

I know you in my body.
 My body knows you.
My body has always known you.
  The first few years, I didn't know
  that it was you
  that my body was knowing,
  but you have never not been there.

I know the way I know you
is not the way
I was told I would know you.
  You are not a thought
  or a concept or a belief,
  or even an emotion, or an insight,
  and my body knows you.

I can touch those parts of my body
which know you best
  in which you seem to dwell.
I can even give names
to some of the qualities
of the experience
  of knowing you in my body,
  and because I know you in my body,
  there is no possible denying of knowing you.

My eyes are your eyes;
and so when I look at myself,
when I reflect upon myself,
when I consider myself,
it is at the same time
that you are seeing me.

And what do you want?
You want to be God,
and you are God by becoming.
And how do you become?
"In and through me…" and everywhere else,
and through everything that lives and breathes,
and through everything that is.

And what is it for you
to become yourself through me?
What is it for me to allow you,
to woo you,
into existence?
It is simply this:
my life
and all the unbearable dilemmas and paradoxes
of human living
are, in fact,
the forge you are becoming.
I know you not to be the cure for anything.

It seems that we have invented
a variety of fabricated realities,
each with their own

so-called diseases
for which you are
the supposed cure.
You do not save me from life
or any of the dilemmas of life.

Rather, life is you, my life is you,
the horrors of my life give you birth,
and you need me to love you enough
to allow that to happen,
and I do
I will suffer my suffering
which is your birthing
because I am moved
in your willingness
to suffer your suffering
so that you may be God.
And I know
that in the suffering of my suffering,
I join with you.

Notes

○○○○○○○○○○○○○○

Introduction

Page

xv. "From all eternity…" Matthew Fox, *Meditations With Meister Eckhart: A Centering Book* (Santa Fe, NM: Bear & Company, 1982), 88.

xv. "So, it is…" Blanche Gallagher, *Meditations With Teilhard de Chardin: A Centering Book* (Sante Fe, NM: Bear & Company, 1988), 112.

xvi. "Please help God…" Poem of a five-year-old.

I. The Experience of Reality

3. "You have placed…" *An Interrupted Life: The Diaries of Etty Hillesum, 1941-1943* (New York, NY: Washington Square Press, 1985), 208.

4. "Life is difficult…" M. Scott Peck, *The Road Less Traveled: A New Psychology of Love, Traditional Values and Spiritual Growth* (New York, NY: Simon & Schuster, 1978).

5. "I now realize…" *An Interrupted Life: The Diaries of Etty Hillesum, 1941-1943*, Ibid.

6. "I, who live…" Madeleine L'Engle, "Word" in *The Weather of the Heart* (Wheaton, IL: Harold Shaw Publications, 1978), quoted from IONA, Autumn 1993, 15-16.

7. "In the humanity…" Gallagher, *Meditations With Teilhard de Chardin*, Ibid., 140.

15. "For this Law…" Henry Wansbrough, *The New Jerusalem Bible* (Garden City, NY: Doubleday, 1985).

25-26. "Last week the waves…" Michael Dwinell, *My Father's Voice* (Friar Tuck Publishing, 1990).

27. "Suddenly I understood…" John P. Dourley, *The Illness That We Are: A Jungian Critique of Christianity* (Toronto, Canada: Inner City Books, 1984), 95.

33. "The self is…" L'Engle, *The Weather of the Heart*, Ibid, 15-16.

35. "Over every living…" Gallagher, *Meditations With Teilhard de Chardin*, Ibid., 139.

37. "My dreams always…" Marion Woodman, Kate Danson, Mary Hamilton, Rita Greer Allen, *Leaving My Father's House: The Journey to Conscious Femininity* (Boston, MA: Shambhala, 1993), 104.

II. The Denial of Reality

41. "This is not…" C.G. Jung, "The Undiscovered Self", Quoted by John A. Sanford in *Mystical Christianity: A Psychological Commentary on the Gospel of John* (New York, NY: Crossroad Press, 1993).

44. "For these differing…" Dourley, *The Illness That We Are*, Ibid., 17-18.

45. "Thus the full…" Ibid., 11.

47. "The most depressing…" *An Interrupted Life: The Diaries of Etty Hillesum, 1941-1943*, Ibid., 197.

49. "What is hidden…" Thomas Merton, *Bread in the Wilderness* (Collegeville, MN: Liturgical Press, 1986). Quoted by Sanford, *Mystical Christianity*, Ibid., 4. [Quoted from Reinbert Herbert, "The Way of Angels," *Parabola* (Su 1989): 86]

51. "Tillich could thus…" Dourley, *The Illness That We Are*, Ibid., 33.

53. "Forgive us, O Lord…" T. S. Elliot, *Murder in the Cathedral: The Complete Poems and Plays, 1909-1950* (New York, NY: Harcourt Brace & Co., 1971), 221.

55. "Instead of considering…" Dourley, *The Illness That We Are*, Ibid., 96.

58. "It would mean…" Ibid., 40.

59. "For it clearly…" John P. Dourley, *A Strategy for a Loss of Faith: Jung's Proposal* (Toronto, Canada: Inner City Books, 1992), 133.

61. "However, conventional religion…" Sanford, *Mystical Christianity*, Ibid., 152.

63. "For the Cry…" Nikos Kazantzakis, *The Rock Garden* (New York NY: Simon & Schuster, 1963), 222-223.

III. Reality as the Tension of the Opposites

68. "Search the darkness…" Jelaluddin Rumi, *Love Is a Stranger*, Translated by Kabir Helminski, "Search the Darkness" (Putney, VT: Threshold Books, 1993), 37.

71. "We are conditioned…" Robert A. Johnson, *Transformation: Understanding the Three Levels of Masculine Consciousness* (San Francisco, CA: HarperCollins, 1991), 59.

72. "Dear Frau Frobe…" Gerhard Adler and Aniela Jaffe, Editors, *C. G. Jung Letters, Volume 1: 1906-1950*, Translated from the German by R.F.C. Hull. In two volumes. I:1906-1950 (Princeton, NJ: Princeton University Press. 1973), Bollingen Series XCV:I, 375.

74. "By coming to terms…" *An Interrupted Life: The Diaries of Etty Hillesum, 1941-1942*, Ibid., 162.

77. "The solution must…" Robert A. Johnson, *Owning Your Own Shadow: Understanding the Dark Side of the Psyche* (San Francisco, CA: HarperCollins, 1993), 87.

79. "In a showdown…" Robert A. Johnson, *Owning Your Own Shadow: Understanding the Dark Side of the Psyche*, Ibid., [Quoted from John Sanford, *The Strange Trial of Dr. Hyde* (San Francisco, CA: Harper & Row, 1987)], 45.

81. "Some of the pure..." Ibid., 7.

82-83. "As a small..." An account of this dream also appears in Michael Dwinell, *Fire Bearer,* "The Apple and the Needle" (Liguori, MO: Triumph Books, Liguori Publications, 1993), 126.

84. "Do you remember..." Robert A. Johnson, *Owning Your Own Shadow: Understanding the Dark Side of the Psyche,* Ibid., 107.

88. "I am Yahweh..." Wansbrough, *The New Jerusalem Bible,* Ibid., Isaiah 45:6.

89. "If Rudolf Otto..." Sanford, *Mystical Christianity,* Ibid., 151.

91. "See now that I..." Wansbrough, *The New Jerusalem Bible,* Deuteronomy 32:39.

92. "God needs humanity..." Dourley, *The Illness That We Are,* Ibid., 54.

95. "...as the conscious..." C.G. Jung, "Two Essays on Analytical Society," Quoted from front plate of Eugene Monick, *Evil, Sexuality and Disease in Grunewald's Body of Christ* (Dallas, TX: Spring Publications, 1993).

96. "How ever great..." Matthew Fox, *Meditations With Meister Eckhart: A Centering Book,* Ibid., 101.

98. "More and more..." Harry T. Moore, *Selected Letters of Rainer Maria Rilke* (Garden City, NY: Doubleday, 1960), 352-353.

100. "Does your heart..." Matthew Fox, *Meditations With Meister Eckhart: A Centering Book,* Ibid., 88.

102. "Although it is..." Gerald G. May, *The Awakened Heart: Living Beyond Addiction* (San Francisco, CA: Harper SF, 1991), 103.

104. "The Word of God..." Matthew Fox, *Meditations With Meister Eckhart: A Centering Book,* Ibid., 72.

105. "When I wake..." Katherine Butler Hathaway, *The Journals and Letters of the Little Locksmith* (Coward-McCann, 1946), 385.

106. "For suffering smashes..." Ken Wilber, *No Boundary: Eastern and Western Approaches to Personal Growth* (Boston, MA: Shambahala Publications, Inc., 1979), 85.

108. "Much of his…" Dourley, *The Illness That We Are*, Ibid., 99.

112. "The need to…" Ibid., 95.

IV. *Empathy and Compassion*

117. "And if God…" *An Interrupted Life: The Diaries of Etty Hillesum, 1941-1943*, Ibid., 181.

118. "I shall try…" Ibid., 187.

118. "There is, in truth…" Gallagher, *Meditations With Teilhard de Chardin*, Ibid., 102.

120. "Faith would be…" Annie Dillard, *Holy the Firm* (Harper & Row, 1977), 47.

121. "Both would agree…" Dourley, *A Strategy for a Loss of Faith: Jung's Proposal*, Ibid., 132.

122. "I shall have…" *An Interrupted Life: The Diaries of Etty Hillesum, 1941-1943*, Ibid., 231.

127. "In his Calcutta…" John Howard Griffin, *Follow the Ecstasy: The Hermitage Years of Thomas Merton* (Maryknoll, NY: Orbis Books, 1993), 151.

128. "We are all…" Gallagher, *Meditations With Teilhard de Chardin*, Ibid., 131.

129. "From the human…" Dourley, *A Strategy for a Loss of Faith: Jung's Proposal*, Ibid., 130.

131-3. "Given the lambs…" Denise Levertov, "Mass for the Day of St. Thomas Dydimus" from *Candles in Babylon* (New York, NY: New Directions, 1982), 113.

137. "I am more…" Gallagher, *Meditations With Teilhard de Chardin*, Ibid., 122.

139-140. "From the conservative…" Edward Mendelson, Editor, *Selected Poems of W.H. Auden* (New York, NY: Vintage Books, 1979), 88-89.

143. "Rather here Jung's…" Dourley, *A Strategy for a Loss of Faith: Jung's Proposal*, Ibid., 121.

144-5. "We sat together…" Susan Griffin, *Chorus of Stones: The Private Life of War* (New York, NY: Anchor, Doubleday Books, 1993), 102-103.

146. "The powers that…" Gallagher, *Meditations With Teilhard de Chardin*, Ibid., 119.

151. "Jung sums this up…" Dourley, *A Strategy for a Loss of Faith: Jung's Proposal*, Ibid., 125.

153. "I embark on…" *An Interrupted Life: The Diaries of Etty Hillesum, 1941-1943*, Ibid., 215.

156. "Up until now…" Gallagher, *Meditations With Teilhard de Chardin*, Ibid., 129.

157. "I so wish…" *An Interrupted Life: the Diaries of Etty Hillesum, 1941-1943*, Ibid., 215.

158. "When I suffer…" Ibid., 242.

159. "I shall merely…" Ibid., 183.

Bibliography

ooooooooooooooo

Adler, Gerhard and Aniela Jaffe, Editors. *C.G. Jung Letters, Volume 1: 1906-1950.* Translated from the German by R.F.C. Hull. In two volumes. I:1906-1950. Bollingen Series. Princeton, NJ: Princeton University Press. 1973.

An Interrupted Life: The Diaries of Etty Hillesum, 1941-1943. New York, NY: Washington Square Press. 1985.

Boas, George. *The Cult of Childhood.* Dallas, TX: Spring Publications, Inc. 1966.

Brueggemann, Walter. *The Prophetic Imagination.* Philadelphia, PA: Augsburg Fortress Press. 1978.

Dillard, Annie. *Holy the Firm.* New York, NY: HarperCollins. 1988.

Dourley, John P. *A Strategy for a Loss of Faith: Jung's Proposal.* Toronto, Canada: Inner City Books. 1992.

———. *The Illness That We Are: A Jungian Critique of Christianity.* Toronto, Canada: Inner City Books. 1984.

Dwinell, Michael. *Fire Bearer.* Liguori, MO: Triumph Books. 1993.

————. *My Father's Voice.* Friar Tuck Publishing. 1990.

Edinger, Edward F. *Transformation of the God Image.* Toronto, Canada: Inner City Books. 1992.

Elliot, T. S. *Murder in the Cathedral: The Complete Poems and Plays, 1909-1950.* New York, NY: Harcourt Brace & Co. 1971.

Fox, Matthew. *Meditations With Meister Eckhart: A Centering Book.* Santa Fe, NM: Bear & Company. 1982.

Gallagher, Blanche. *Meditations With Teilhard de Chardin: A Centering Book.* Sante Fe, NM: Bear & Company. 1988.

Gergen, Kenneth J. *Saturated Self: Dilemmas of Identity in Contemporary Life.* New York, NY: Basic Books. 1981.

Griffin, John Howard. *Follow the Ecstasy: The Hermitage Years of Thomas Merton.* Maryknoll, NY: Orbis Books. 1993.

Hathaway, Katherine Butler. *The Journals and Letters of the Little Locksmith.* Coward-McCann. 1946.

Hillman, James and Michael Ventura. *We've Had a Hundred Years of Psychotherapy—and the World's Getting Worse.* San Francisco, CA: Harper SF. 1992.

Johnson, Robert A. *Owning Your Own Shadow: Understanding the Dark Side of the Psyche.* New York, NY: HarperCollins. 1991.

————. *Transformation: Understanding the Three Levels of Masculine Consciousness.* New York, NY: HarperCollins. 1991.

Kazantzakis, Nikos. *The Rock Garden.* New York NY: Simon & Schuster. 1963.

Kramer, Victor A. *Thomas Merton: Monk and Artist.* Kalamazoo, MI: Cistercian Publications. 1988.

Lawrence, David H. *St. Mawr and the Man Who Died.* New York, NY: Vintage Books. 1953.

L'Engle, Madeleine. *The Weather of the Heart.* Wheaton, IL: Harold Shaw Publications. 1978.

Levertov, Denise. *Candles in Babylon.* New York, NY: New Directions. 1982.

May, Gerald G. *The Awakened Heart: Living Beyond Addiction.* San Francisco, CA: Harper SF. 1991.

Mendelson, Edward. Editor. *Selected Poems of W.H. Auden.* New York, NY: Vintage Books. 1979.

Mitchell, Stephen. Editor. *The Enlightened Heart.* New York, NY: HarperCollins. 1992.

Monick, Eugene. *Evil, Sexuality and Disease in Grunewald's Body of Christ.* Dallas, TX: Spring Publications. 1993.

Moore, Harry T. *Selected Letters of Rainer Maria Rilke.* Garden City, NY: Doubleday. 1960.

Moore, Thomas. *Dark Eros: The Imagination of Sadism.* Dallas, TX: Spring Publications, Inc. 1990.

————. *Soulmates: Honoring the Mysteries of Love and Relationship.* New York, NY: HarperCollins. 1994.

Peck, M. Scott. *The Road Less Traveled: A New Psychology of Love, Traditional Values and Spiritual Growth.* New York, NY: Simon and Schuster. 1978.

Perry, John W. *The Far Side of Madness.* Dallas, TX: Spring Publications, Inc. 1974.

Rumi, Jelaluddin. *Love Is a Stranger.* Translated by Kabir Helminski. Putney, VT: Threshold Books. 1993.

Sanford, John A. *Mystical Christianity: A Psychological Commentary on the Gospel of John*. New York, NY: Crossroad Press. 1993.

Shea, John. *Stories of Faith.* Chicago, IL: Thomas Moore Press. 1980.

Wilber, Ken. *No Boundary: Eastern and Western Approaches to Personal Growth*. Boston, MA: Shambahala Publications, Inc. 1979.

Woodman, Marion with Kate Danson, Mary Hamilton, Rita Greer Allen. *Leaving My Father's House: The Journey to Conscious Femininity*. Boston, MA: Shambhala. 1993.